For prize giveaways, free content, book giveaways, and more please email us and tell us you want to be included on our email list.

Visit us online at

www.touchtheskypublishing.com

Check us out on Instagram
@touchtheskypublishing

TOUCHTHESKYPUBLISHINC

https://www.instagram.com/
touchtheskypublishing/

Check us out on twitter
@touchtheskybook

https://twitter.com/
touchtheskybook

Check us out on Facebook
@Touchtheskypublishing

https://www.facebook.com/
Touchtheskypublishing

www.Touchtheskypublishing.com

INTRODUCTION

In a world of limitless opportunities, the pursuit of financial freedom has taken on a new dimension. As the traditional 9-to-5 job landscape evolves, more and more individuals are seeking ways to bolster their income and secure their financial future.

This book is your guide to the side hustles, designed to help you navigate the waves toward your financial goals. Whether you dream of paying off debt, building an emergency fund, saving for a vacation, or even achieving financial independence, this guide will provide you with the knowledge and inspiration you need to set sail.

Inside these pages, you will discover a treasure trove of side hustle opportunities that are waiting for you to explore.

But "Make Money Now" is not just a list of money-making ideas. It's a comprehensive road map that will lead you through the entire process, from choosing the right side hustle to launching it successfully.

We understand that your time is valuable, so we've done the research, analyzed the trends, and gathered insights from successful side hustlers.

Whether you're a stay-at-home parent, a full-time employee looking to supplement your income, a student trying to make ends meet, or an aspiring entrepreneur dipping your toes into the world of business, there's a side hustle in this book that's tailor-made for you.

So, are you ready to embark on this exciting journey? Are you prepared to seize the opportunities that can transform your financial landscape and bring you one step closer to your dreams? "Make Money Now" is your key to unlocking the doors of financial prosperity. Your financial success story begins now.

ROLLING BILLBOARD

Turning Your Car into a Rolling Billboard: Earning Extra Money Through Car Advertising

In today's gig economy, individuals are finding creative ways to supplement their income. One innovative approach is turning your car into a mobile advertising platform, allowing businesses to promote their products or services while you earn extra cash. In this page, we'll explore the world of car advertising, its benefits, how it works, and considerations before jumping on board.

What Is Car Advertising?

Car advertising, also known as vehicle advertising or car wrapping, involves placing advertisements or branding materials on your car's exterior. This form of advertising allows businesses to reach a broader audience while compensating car owners for using their vehicles as mobile billboards. It's a win-win arrangement that leverages the visibility of vehicles to promote products or services.

Benefits of Car Advertising

Extra Income: Car advertising provides a passive income stream, allowing you to earn money while going about your daily activities.

Minimal Effort: Once your car is wrapped or adorned with advertisements, there's little ongoing effort required on your part.

No Fixed Commitment: Car advertising is typically a short-term commitment, and you can choose the campaigns and companies you work with.

Free Car Maintenance: Some car advertising agreements may cover vehicle maintenance and repairs, further reducing your expenses.

Visibility: Your car becomes a moving billboard, increasing the visibility of the advertiser's brand.

How Car Advertising Works

Application: Car owners interested in car advertising apply for campaigns through advertising agencies or online platforms that connect advertisers with drivers.

Approval: Once accepted, you'll receive instructions on how to have your car wrapped or adorned with decals. The process is usually handled by professionals to ensure the quality of the ad placement.

Driving as Usual: After your car is wrapped or decorated, you can drive as usual. There's no need to alter your daily routines.

Payment: Car advertisers compensate drivers based on various factors, such as the campaign duration, the size of the ad, and the location where you drive. Payments can be made weekly, monthly, or as specified in the agreement.

Campaign Duration: Car advertising campaigns can range from a few months to a year or more, depending on the advertiser's goals.

Considerations Before Participating in Car Advertising

Vehicle Condition: Your car should be in good condition and well-maintained before applying for car advertising. Advertisers often require vehicles that look clean and presentable.

Driving Habits: Consider your daily driving habits and routes. Some advertisers may have specific requirements regarding the areas where your car should be driven.

Duration Commitment: Be sure you're comfortable with the campaign duration and any contractual obligations.

Privacy Concerns: Car advertising may involve tracking your driving patterns for campaign analysis. Ensure you're comfortable with the level of data sharing required.

Local Regulations: Check local regulations and permits, as some areas may have restrictions or requirements for car advertising.

Car advertising offers an innovative and convenient way to earn extra money while using your vehicle as a mobile billboard. It's a flexible gig that can fit into your daily routine and provide a steady income stream. As with any opportunity, it's essential to consider your personal preferences, vehicle condition, and the terms of the advertising agreement before embarking on this journey. If you're looking for a creative way to boost your income without major lifestyle changes, car advertising might just be the ticket.

SUBSTITUTE TEACHING

Substitute teaching is a dynamic and essential role within the education system, bridging the gap when regular teachers are absent. It offers individuals the opportunity to make a meaningful impact on students' lives while enjoying a flexible and rewarding career. In this page, we'll explore the world of substitute teaching, its responsibilities, the challenges it presents, and the financial aspects, including the pay range.

The Role of a Substitute Teacher

Substitute teachers are the unsung heroes of the education system, stepping into classrooms to ensure that the learning process continues seamlessly. Their responsibilities include:

Facilitating Learning: Substitute teachers deliver pre-planned lessons or manage classroom activities, maintaining educational progress during a teacher's absence.

Classroom Management: They establish a positive learning environment, enforce classroom rules, and manage student behavior.

Lesson Execution: Substitute teachers follow lesson plans and instructions provided by regular teachers, ensuring that the curriculum is covered.

Adaptability: They must be adaptable, as they may teach different subjects, grade levels, or classrooms on short notice.

Communication: Effective communication with students, staff, and parents is vital to address concerns and provide updates.

Qualities of an Effective Substitute Teacher

Successful substitute teachers possess certain qualities that enable them to excel in their role:

Flexibility: The ability to adapt to different teaching styles, grade levels, and subjects is crucial.

Classroom Management: They must establish and maintain a positive classroom environment conducive to learning.

Communication Skills: Effective communication with students, staff, and parents is essential.

Organization: Good organizational skills help substitute teachers manage lesson plans, classroom materials, and schedules efficiently.

Patience: Dealing with diverse student behaviors and needs requires patience and understanding.

Problem-Solving: Quick thinking and problem-solving abilities are vital in handling unexpected situations.

Challenges in Substitute Teaching

Substitute teaching comes with its set of challenges:

Limited Preparation: Substitute teachers often receive limited information about the classroom, students, and curriculum before arriving.

Diverse Student Needs: They must adapt to different grade levels, subjects, and student populations, each with unique needs and challenges.

Classroom Management: Managing student behavior and maintaining discipline can be challenging in an unfamiliar classroom.

Continual Change: Substitute teachers frequently move between schools and may not have a consistent teaching environment.

Lack of Benefits: Many substitute teachers work without the benefits or job security that regular teachers receive.

Rewards of Substitute Teaching
While substitute teaching presents its challenges, it offers numerous rewards:

Impact on Students: Substitute teachers can make a positive impact on students' lives by providing continuity in their education.

Variety: The opportunity to work in different schools and classrooms offers variety and professional growth.

Flexibility: Substitute teaching provides flexibility, allowing individuals to balance work with other responsibilities.

Path to Full Teaching: Some substitute teachers use the role as a stepping stone toward full-time teaching positions.

Contribution to Education: Substitute teachers contribute to the overall functioning of the education system and student success.

Pay Range for Substitute Teachers
The pay for substitute teachers can vary significantly depending on factors like location, level of education, and the school district. In the United States, as of my last knowledge update in September 2021, the average substitute teacher's hourly pay ranged from approximately $10 to $30 per hour. Some districts offer daily rates, which can vary from $60 to $150 or more per day. It's important to note that long-term substitute positions or those requiring specialized skills may offer higher pay rates. Additionally, substitute teachers with teaching credentials or certifications may command higher compensation.

Substitute teaching is a valuable and fulfilling career path that empowers individuals to contribute to education while enjoying flexibility in their work. Despite the challenges, substitute teachers play an essential role in maintaining the continuity of learning and supporting the development of students. If you're passionate about education and seek a rewarding and dynamic career, substitute teaching may be the ideal choice for you.

FREELANCING

Freelancing: Unlocking the World of Independent Work

In recent years, the world of work has undergone a significant transformation, with the rise of freelancing taking center stage. Freelancing, often referred to as the gig economy, has evolved into a dynamic and accessible way for individuals to earn income, offering newfound freedom and flexibility.

The Freelancer's Odyssey

Freelancing is not a new concept. Historically, artisans, writers, and tradespeople have been working independently for centuries. However, in the digital age, the opportunities for freelancers have expanded exponentially. Today, anyone with a marketable skill, from writing and design to programming and consulting, can embark on their own freelancing journey.

Why Freelance?

The appeal of freelancing lies in its numerous advantages. Here are some compelling reasons why many individuals choose to embrace this mode of work:

Flexibility: Freelancers have the freedom to set their own schedules and choose their projects. This flexibility allows for a better work-life balance.

Diverse Opportunities: Freelancers can work across various industries and projects, gaining a wealth of experience and expanding their skill sets.

Independence: Freelancers are their own bosses. They have the autonomy to make decisions and shape their careers.

Income Potential: Depending on the skill set and demand for services, freelancers often have the potential to earn a competitive income.

Global Reach: The internet has made it possible for freelancers to work with clients and businesses from around the world, broadening their horizons and opportunities.

The Gig Economy's Backbone

Freelancing spans a wide range of professions, making it accessible to individuals with diverse skill sets. Here are some of the most common freelance categories:

Content Creation: Freelance writers, bloggers, and content creators provide written and visual content for websites, blogs, and social media.

Design and Multimedia: Graphic designers, illustrators, and video editors offer creative services for branding, marketing, and entertainment.

Web Development and Programming: Freelancers in this category create websites, apps, and software programs for businesses and individuals.

Consulting and Coaching: Freelance consultants, coaches, and advisors offer expertise in areas like business, career, and personal development.

Marketing and SEO: Freelancers in this field help businesses with digital marketing, search engine optimization (SEO), and advertising campaigns.

Admin and Virtual Assistance: Virtual assistants and administrative freelancers provide support services to businesses, including email management, data entry, and scheduling.

Navigating the Freelance Landscape

While freelancing offers many benefits, it also comes with its own set of challenges. Freelancers must be self-disciplined, manage their finances, handle client relationships, and continually market their services. Building a successful freelancing career often requires a combination of skills beyond the core service being offered.

Platforms and Marketplaces

To connect with clients and find freelance opportunities, many individuals turn to online platforms and marketplaces. Websites like Upwork, Freelancer, Fiverr, and Toptal act as intermediaries, matching freelancers with clients seeking specific services. These platforms provide access to a global network of potential clients, making it easier for freelancers to find work.

Freelance Success Stories

Numerous success stories abound in the world of freelancing. Individuals who started as independent freelancers have gone on to build thriving businesses, agencies, and brands. Freelancing has enabled many to pursue their passions, travel the world, and achieve financial independence.

Freelancing has emerged as a dynamic and viable career option in today's ever-evolving job market. Whether you're a recent graduate, a stay-at-home parent, or a seasoned professional, freelancing offers an opportunity to take control of your career, explore your passions, and unlock a world of independent work. As the gig economy continues to grow, freelancers are poised to play a pivotal role in shaping the future of work.

SELLING ON ETSY

Etsy: Empowering Artisans and Crafters to Share Their Passion

Etsy is a vibrant online marketplace that has redefined how artisans and crafters connect with a global audience to sell their handmade crafts and art. In this page, we will explore the world of selling handmade creations on Etsy, including its significance, the process, tips for success, and the potential income artisans can earn.

The Significance of Etsy

Etsy has become an invaluable platform for creative individuals seeking to turn their artistic talents into a thriving business. Its significance lies in several key areas:

Empowering Creativity: Etsy empowers artisans and crafters to transform their creative passions into a source of income. It offers a space where unique and handmade items are celebrated and valued.

Accessibility: The platform is accessible to artists worldwide, regardless of their location or prior experience in e-commerce. This democratization of online selling enables anyone with artistic skills to participate.

Community: Etsy fosters a sense of community among sellers and buyers. Artisans can connect with like-minded individuals, share ideas, and receive support from a global network of creative entrepreneurs.

Global Reach: Etsy provides a global audience for artisans' work, allowing them to reach customers from around the world who appreciate and seek one-of-a-kind, handcrafted items.

How Selling on Etsy Works

Selling handmade crafts and art on Etsy involves a straightforward process:

Create an Etsy Shop: Begin by setting up your Etsy shop. This involves choosing a shop name, adding product listings, and configuring shop policies, such as shipping and returns.

Product Listings: Create appealing product listings for your handmade items. Include high-quality photos, detailed descriptions, pricing, and shipping information to attract potential buyers.

Payment and Shipping: Configure your preferred payment methods and shipping options. Etsy offers various payment gateways and calculates shipping costs based on location.

Shop Promotion: Actively promote your shop and products through social media, email marketing, and Etsy's advertising tools. Utilize Etsy's built-in SEO features to enhance your shop's visibility in search results.

Fulfilling Orders: When orders come in, carefully package your products and ship them to customers. Etsy offers convenient shipping labels and tracking options to streamline the process.

Customer Engagement: Maintain open communication with customers, promptly address inquiries, and provide excellent service to build a positive reputation.

Tips for Success on Etsy

Success on Etsy requires a combination of creative talent and effective selling strategies. Here are some essential tips to elevate your Etsy shop:

Quality and Originality: Craft high-quality, original items that stand out in the market. Unique creations are more likely to attract buyers.

Photography Skills: Invest time in capturing professional-quality product photos that showcase your items' details and craftsmanship.

Engaging Descriptions: Write informative and engaging product descriptions that convey the story and uniqueness of each item.

Competitive Pricing: Research competitors and consider materials, labor, and overhead costs when pricing your products.

Customer-Centric Approach: Provide exceptional customer service, respond to inquiries promptly, and address any issues professionally and courteously.

Consistent Branding: Maintain a consistent visual identity and branding throughout your shop to create a cohesive and memorable shopping experience.

Expand Your Product Line: Continuously introduce new items to your shop to keep customers engaged and encourage repeat business.

Potential Income on Etsy

Earning potential on Etsy varies widely based on factors such as the type of products you sell, your pricing strategy, marketing efforts, and the demand for your creations. Some artisans may earn a supplemental income, while others have turned their Etsy shops into full-time businesses.

On average, Etsy sellers can earn anywhere from a few hundred to several thousand dollars per month, with top-performing shops achieving even higher income levels. It's essential to set realistic expectations and be prepared to invest time and effort into building and promoting your shop to achieve your desired income goals.

Selling handmade crafts and art on Etsy is not just a business endeavor; it's a journey of artistic expression and entrepreneurship. Etsy provides a supportive platform where artisans and crafters can turn their creative passions into a sustainable source of income while connecting with a global community of art enthusiasts. Whether you're an established artist or just starting your creative venture, Etsy offers a welcoming space to share your artistry with the world.

SIGNING AGENT

The Vital Role of a Signing Agent in the World of Documents

A signing agent is a pivotal figure in the world of legal and financial documents. Their expertise in notarizing documents and overseeing signings ensures the integrity of transactions and protects all parties involved. In this page, we will delve into the role of a signing agent, their significance, responsibilities, challenges, and the compensation they can expect.

The Significance of a Signing Agent

The role of a signing agent is significant for several reasons:

Document Verification: Signing agents verify the identity of individuals signing documents, ensuring the legality and authenticity of the signatures.

Transaction Integrity: They play a crucial role in maintaining the integrity of transactions, especially in real estate, by confirming that all parties understand and agree to the terms of the documents they are signing.

Legal Compliance: Signing agents ensure that documents comply with state and federal regulations, reducing the risk of fraud and disputes.

Trust and Confidence: Their presence instills trust and confidence in the signing process, reassuring all parties that their interests are protected.

Responsibilities of a Signing Agent

The responsibilities of a signing agent may vary depending on the type of documents and transactions they handle, but generally include:

Document Verification: Confirming the identity of signers by checking their identification documents.

Notarization: Administering oaths and notarizing documents as required by law.

Witnessing Signatures: Ensuring that all required parties sign documents and that signatures are genuine.

Explaining Documents: Clarifying the purpose and content of the documents being signed, ensuring that signers understand their implications.

Document Handling: Safeguarding sensitive documents and ensuring they are securely delivered to the appropriate parties.

Completing Certificates: Filling out notarial certificates and logs accurately.

Challenges in the Role of a Signing Agent

While the role of a signing agent is essential, it comes with its share of challenges:

Legal Knowledge: Staying up-to-date with changing laws and regulations is crucial for compliance.

Client Communication: Effective communication with clients and signers is essential, especially in complex transactions.

Accuracy: Precision in document handling, notarization, and record-keeping is vital to avoid legal issues.

Time Sensitivity: Some transactions may require rapid response times, making time management crucial.

Compensation for Signing Agents

The compensation for signing agents varies based on factors such as location, experience, and the complexity of the transactions they handle. Signing agents can earn fees for each signing they conduct, which can range from $75 to $200 or more per signing, depending on the complexity.

Some signing agents also charge travel fees for covering long distances to meet clients. Additionally, signing agents can earn extra income by offering services such as document preparation or loan signing, which often command higher fees.

A signing agent's role is vital in the world of legal and financial documents, ensuring the legality and integrity of transactions. Their responsibilities encompass document verification, notarization, and facilitating smooth signings. While the role comes with its challenges, signing agents are compensated fairly for their expertise, with earning potential varying based on location and experience. Ultimately, signing agents provide a crucial service that safeguards the interests of all parties involved in important transactions.

MOBILE NOTARY

Mobile Notary Services: Bringing Notarization to Your Doorstep

Mobile notary services have emerged as a convenient and flexible solution for individuals and businesses in need of notarized documents. By offering on-the-go notarization, mobile notaries bring their expertise directly to clients, saving time and simplifying the often complex process of document authentication. In this page, we will explore the world of mobile notary services, their significance, responsibilities, challenges, and the compensation they can expect.

The Significance of Mobile Notary Services

Mobile notary services have become increasingly significant in our fast-paced and interconnected world. Their importance lies in several key areas:

Accessibility: Mobile notaries make notarization services accessible to individuals and businesses who may have difficulty visiting a physical notary's office during regular business hours.

Convenience: They provide the convenience of notarization at a location and time that suits the client, whether it's a home, office, hospital room, or another preferred venue.

Flexibility: Mobile notaries are adaptable, catering to a wide range of notarial needs, from real estate closings and legal documents to affidavits and wills.

Document Authentication: They play a critical role in ensuring the authenticity of signatures and documents, reducing the risk of fraud and disputes.

Responsibilities of a Mobile Notary

The responsibilities of a mobile notary are similar to those of traditional notaries, with the added flexibility of location:

Document Verification: Confirming the identity of individuals signing documents by checking their identification documents.

Notarization: Administering oaths and notarizing documents as required by law.

Witnessing Signatures: Ensuring that all required parties sign documents and that signatures are genuine.

Explaining Documents: Clarifying the purpose and content of the documents being signed, ensuring that signers understand their implications.

Document Handling: Safeguarding sensitive documents and maintaining the confidentiality of client information.

Record-Keeping: Accurately completing notarial certificates and maintaining detailed records of notarized transactions.

Challenges in the Role of a Mobile Notary

While mobile notaries offer convenience, they also face unique challenges:

Client Scheduling: Coordinating appointments at various locations can be challenging, especially when clients have busy schedules.

Travel Time: Mobile notaries often spend considerable time traveling between appointments.

Privacy and Security: Safeguarding client information and ensuring the security of notarized documents is crucial.

Compensation for Mobile Notaries

The compensation for mobile notaries varies based on factors such as location, experience, and the complexity of the notarization. Mobile notaries typically charge fees for each notarization they perform, which can range from $25 to $75 or more per notarization. Additionally, they may charge travel fees, with rates determined by distance and travel time.

Mobile notaries also have the opportunity to offer additional services, such as document preparation or loan signing, which often command higher fees. Overall, the income potential for mobile notaries can be substantial, particularly for those who build a solid client base and offer specialized services.

Mobile notary services have become an indispensable part of our modern world, providing accessibility and convenience in the notarization process. Mobile notaries carry out responsibilities similar to traditional notaries but with the added flexibility of location and scheduling. While they face challenges related to client coordination and document security, mobile notaries are compensated fairly for their expertise, offering a valuable service that simplifies the often complex world of document authentication.

DAY TRADING

Day Trading: Navigating the World of Rapid-Fire Financial Markets

Day trading is a high-stakes venture within the financial world, where individuals seek to profit from the short-term price movements of stocks, commodities, currencies, or other financial instruments. This fast-paced trading style involves buying and selling positions within the same trading day, often multiple times. In this page, we'll explore the world of day trading, its significance, strategies, responsibilities, challenges, and the potential compensation involved.

The Significance of Day Trading

Day trading holds significance in the financial industry for several reasons:

Market Liquidity: Day traders contribute to market liquidity by executing frequent trades, helping ensure that buyers and sellers can easily transact.

Price Efficiency: Their active participation aids in establishing fair market prices by taking advantage of short-term price discrepancies.

Speculation and Profits: Day trading provides an opportunity for individuals to speculate on price movements and potentially generate profits in a relatively short timeframe.

Day Trading Strategies

Day traders employ a variety of strategies to make quick profits, including:

Scalping: Profiting from small price fluctuations by executing a large number of trades within a single day.

Trend Following: Identifying and capitalizing on existing price trends, whether upward or downward.

Range Trading: Buying at the low end and selling at the high end of a trading range.

Contrarian Trading: Betting against the prevailing market sentiment, assuming that trends will reverse.

Algorithmic Trading: Using automated trading software to execute a large number of trades based on pre-defined algorithms.

Responsibilities of a Day Trader

Day traders bear several responsibilities:

Research and Analysis: Conducting thorough research and analysis of stocks or other assets to identify potential trading opportunities.

Risk Management: Implementing risk management strategies to limit potential losses and protect capital.

Trade Execution: Timely and accurate execution of trades, often in a fast-paced environment.

Record Keeping: Maintaining detailed records of all trades and strategies for tax purposes and performance evaluation.

Emotional Discipline: Maintaining emotional discipline to avoid impulsive decisions driven by fear or greed.

Challenges in Day Trading

Day trading comes with its fair share of challenges:

High Risk: The potential for significant financial losses is high, especially for inexperienced traders.

Emotional Stress: The fast-paced nature of day trading can lead to stress, anxiety, and emotional burnout.

Knowledge and Skill: Successful day trading requires a deep understanding of markets, strategies, and financial instruments.

Regulatory Compliance: Adherence to financial regulations and compliance requirements is crucial.

Compensation in Day Trading

The compensation in day trading is highly variable and depends on several factors, including:

Experience: Experienced day traders with a proven track record can earn substantial income.

Capital: The amount of capital invested in trading significantly impacts potential earnings.

Skill and Strategy: Effective trading strategies and decision-making skills contribute to profitability.

Market Conditions: Market volatility and conditions can influence daily earnings.

Day traders may earn anywhere from a few hundred dollars to several thousand dollars per day, with top traders potentially earning millions annually. However, it's important to note that the majority of day traders do not achieve consistent profits and may incur losses.

Day trading is a challenging and high-risk endeavor that offers the potential for significant financial rewards. It plays a vital role in financial markets by contributing to liquidity and price efficiency. While successful day traders can earn substantial income, it requires a deep understanding of markets, effective strategies, emotional discipline, and the ability to manage risk. For those who thrive in this fast-paced environment, day trading can be a rewarding and potentially lucrative career.

YOUTUBE

Creating Content and Earning on YouTube: Turning Passion into Profit

YouTube has revolutionized the way people consume content and provided creators with a platform to share their creativity, knowledge, and passions with a global audience. For many, YouTube offers not only a creative outlet but also a means of generating income. In this page, we will explore the world of YouTube content creation, its significance, strategies, responsibilities, challenges, and the potential compensation involved.

The Significance of YouTube

YouTube is significant in several ways:

Global Reach: It provides creators with access to a global audience of billions, transcending geographical boundaries.

Diverse Content: YouTube hosts a vast range of content, from educational tutorials and entertainment to vlogs and product reviews, catering to a wide array of interests.

Monetization: It offers content creators opportunities to monetize their channels through various income streams.

Community Building: Creators can build engaged communities of subscribers who share their interests and engage with their content.

Content Creation Strategies

Successful YouTubers often employ the following strategies:

Niche Selection: Identifying a niche or specific area of interest that aligns with their expertise and passion.

Quality Content: Producing high-quality videos with engaging visuals, storytelling, and effective communication.

Consistency: Maintaining a regular upload schedule to keep viewers engaged and informed.

Audience Engagement: Interacting with viewers through comments, community posts, and social media to build a loyal fan base.

Monetization: Exploring various monetization methods, such as ads, sponsorships, merchandise sales, and crowdfunding.

Responsibilities of YouTube Content Creators

YouTube content creators bear several responsibilities:

Content Production: Planning, recording, editing, and uploading videos, ensuring content is well-researched and engaging.

Audience Engagement: Responding to comments, addressing questions, and fostering a positive community.

Monetization Management: Implementing and managing monetization strategies and partnerships.

Promotion and Marketing: Promoting their channel and content through social media and other channels to attract and retain viewers.

Adherence to Policies: Complying with YouTube's policies and guidelines, including copyright and community standards.

Challenges in YouTube Content Creation

Despite its appeal, YouTube content creation presents its own set of challenges:

Competition: The platform is highly competitive, with millions of creators vying for viewers' attention.

Consistency: Maintaining a regular upload schedule can be demanding, requiring dedication and time management.

Monetization Uncertainty: Earning substantial income can be challenging, as it depends on factors like viewer engagement and advertising rates.

Content Quality: Creating high-quality content can be resource-intensive and time-consuming.

Algorithm Changes: YouTube's algorithms and policies can change, affecting content visibility and monetization.

Compensation on YouTube

Earnings on YouTube vary widely depending on factors like niche, audience size, and content quality. Potential income streams for YouTubers include:

Ad Revenue: Creators can earn money through ads displayed on their videos, with income influenced by factors like view count, ad types, and viewer engagement.

Sponsorships: Brands may pay creators to promote their products or services in videos.

Merchandise Sales: Creators can design and sell merchandise related to their channel.

Channel Memberships and Donations: Viewers can support creators through channel memberships and donations.

Affiliate Marketing: Earnings can come from promoting affiliate products or services in video descriptions.

Earnings for established YouTubers can range from thousands to millions of dollars annually. However, it's important to note that many creators do not earn significant income and may rely on multiple income sources to sustain their channels.

YouTube content creation offers individuals a unique opportunity to share their passions and knowledge while potentially earning income. Successful YouTubers combine creativity, dedication, and effective strategies to build engaged communities and generate revenue from various sources. While challenges exist, those who excel in this dynamic field can turn their passion into a profitable and fulfilling career.

AFFILIATE MARKETING

Affiliate Marketing: Unlocking Earnings Through Online Partnerships

In today's digital landscape, affiliate marketing has emerged as a powerful and accessible way to generate income. It offers individuals and businesses the opportunity to collaborate and promote products or services, all while earning commissions. In this page, we will delve into the world of affiliate marketing, exploring what it is, how it works, the benefits it offers, and the pay range.

Understanding Affiliate Marketing

Affiliate marketing is a performance-based marketing strategy in which individuals, known as affiliates or publishers, promote products or services on behalf of businesses or advertisers. These affiliates earn a commission for each sale, click, or action generated through their marketing efforts. It's essentially a partnership between advertisers and promoters, with both parties benefiting from the arrangement.

The Mechanics of Affiliate Marketing

The core components of affiliate marketing include:

Advertisers or Merchants: These are businesses or product/service providers seeking to expand their online presence and sales. They create affiliate programs to attract affiliates.

Affiliates or Publishers: These individuals or entities promote the advertiser's products or services through various marketing channels, such as websites, blogs, social media, email, or paid advertising.

Consumers: The end-users who interact with affiliate marketing content and potentially make a purchase or take a desired action.

Affiliate Networks: These platforms act as intermediaries, connecting advertisers with affiliates. They provide tracking, reporting, and payment services, streamlining the affiliate marketing process.

The Affiliate Marketing Process

Here is a simplified breakdown of how affiliate marketing works:

Joining an Affiliate Program: Affiliates sign up for an affiliate program offered by an advertiser or through an affiliate network. Upon approval, they gain access to unique affiliate links or tracking codes.

Promotion: Affiliates create content that includes their affiliate links, promoting the advertiser's products or services to their target audience. This content can take the form of blog posts, reviews, social media posts, email campaigns, or paid advertisements.

Tracking: When consumers click on an affiliate's unique link and perform a specific action (e.g., making a purchase), the affiliate tracking system records the referral and attributes it to the affiliate.

Earning Commissions: Affiliates earn commissions for the actions generated through their affiliate links, as defined by the advertiser's terms. Commissions can be a percentage of the sale, a fixed fee, or other predetermined criteria.

Payment: Affiliate networks or advertisers typically pay affiliates on a predetermined schedule, such as monthly. Payments can be made via various methods, including checks, direct deposit, or PayPal.

Benefits of Affiliate Marketing

Affiliate marketing offers several advantages:

Extra Income: It provides individuals with an opportunity to earn extra income, making it an accessible side hustle.

Flexibility: Affiliates have the freedom to choose the products or services they promote and the strategies they employ.

Minimal Investment: Starting as an affiliate marketer typically requires minimal investment, especially compared to starting a traditional business.

Scalability: As affiliates gain experience, they can scale their efforts and potentially earn more commissions.

Global Reach: Affiliate marketing allows individuals to work with businesses from around the world, expanding their earning potential.

Pay Range for Affiliate Marketers

The pay range for affiliate marketers can vary significantly depending on factors such as:

Niche: Some niches, like finance or technology, may offer higher commission rates due to the value of the products or services.

Conversion Rates: Affiliates with high conversion rates (the percentage of clicks that result in a sale) tend to earn more.

Product Prices: Promoting high-ticket items can lead to higher commissions.

Traffic Quality: Affiliates who drive high-quality traffic that leads to sales are often rewarded.

Commission Structures: Different affiliate programs offer various commission structures, such as pay-per-sale, pay-per-click, or pay-per-lead.

Experience: Seasoned affiliate marketers tend to earn more as they build their skills and audience.

Affiliate marketers can earn anywhere from a few dollars to thousands of dollars per month, depending on these factors. Some top-tier affiliates generate six-figure incomes annually. It's important to note that while affiliate marketing offers income potential, success often requires dedication, strategic marketing, and ongoing effort.

Affiliate marketing is a versatile and potentially lucrative way to generate income in the digital age. Whether you're looking to earn extra money on the side or build a full-time online business, affiliate marketing offers a pathway to financial success. By understanding the mechanics, benefits, and potential pay range of affiliate marketing, you can embark on a journey to unlock earnings through online partnerships.

AMAZON FBA

Amazon FBA: Transforming E-Commerce with Fulfillment Excellence

Amazon FBA (Fulfillment by Amazon) has revolutionized the world of e-commerce, offering entrepreneurs and businesses a streamlined way to sell products online. By leveraging Amazon's extensive logistics network, sellers can reach a global customer base and benefit from efficient order fulfillment. In this page, we will explore the world of Amazon FBA, its significance, how it works, responsibilities, challenges, and the potential compensation involved.

The Significance of Amazon FBA

Amazon FBA is significant for several reasons:

Global Reach: It allows sellers to tap into Amazon's vast customer base, reaching millions of potential buyers worldwide.

Logistics Expertise: FBA leverages Amazon's expertise in warehousing, packing, and shipping, streamlining the order fulfillment process.

Prime Eligibility: Products fulfilled by Amazon are often eligible for Amazon Prime, increasing their visibility and appeal to Prime members.

Customer Trust: Buyers tend to trust and prefer products that are fulfilled by Amazon due to the reliable and fast shipping options.

How Amazon FBA Works

The process of selling through Amazon FBA involves the following steps:

Product Listing: Sellers create product listings on Amazon, specifying that they will be using FBA for order fulfillment.

Inventory Shipment: Sellers ship their inventory to Amazon's fulfillment centers, where it is stored until sold.

Customer Orders: When customers place orders, Amazon handles order processing, packing, and shipping, including customer service and returns.

Prime and Fast Shipping: FBA products often qualify for Amazon Prime and other fast shipping options, enhancing their marketability.

Storage and Fees: Sellers pay storage fees for the space their inventory occupies in Amazon's fulfillment centers and other fees based on usage.

Responsibilities of Amazon FBA Sellers

While Amazon FBA streamlines many aspects of e-commerce, sellers still have several responsibilities:

Product Selection: Choosing profitable products that meet market demand and align with their business strategy.

Inventory Management: Monitoring inventory levels, restocking, and avoiding long-term storage fees.

Competitive Pricing: Setting competitive prices while factoring in fees and shipping costs.

Customer Service: Managing customer inquiries, returns, and feedback effectively.

Marketing: Promoting their products to stand out in the competitive marketplace.

Challenges in Amazon FBA

Selling on Amazon FBA comes with its own set of challenges:

Competition: The platform is highly competitive, with many sellers offering similar products.

Fees: Amazon charges various fees, including referral fees, fulfillment fees, and storage fees, which can impact profitability.

Inventory Management: Balancing inventory levels to meet demand without overstocking can be challenging.

Customer Reviews: Negative reviews can affect a product's reputation and sales.

Policy Compliance: Staying up-to-date with Amazon's policies and regulations is crucial to avoid account suspension.

Compensation in Amazon FBA

The compensation in Amazon FBA varies widely based on factors such as the product niche, competitive landscape, and seller's strategy. Sellers can earn a percentage of the sale price of their products, minus Amazon's fees. Profit margins can range from a few percentage points to over 50%, depending on the product's niche and demand.

Successful Amazon FBA sellers can generate substantial income, ranging from a few thousand dollars to millions annually. However, achieving profitability often requires effective product selection, pricing strategies, and marketing efforts.

Amazon FBA offers entrepreneurs and businesses an opportunity to thrive in the e-commerce landscape by leveraging Amazon's logistics expertise and customer reach. While challenges exist, those who excel in product selection, inventory management, and customer service can potentially build profitable businesses in this dynamic and ever-expanding online marketplace.

AMAZON KDP

Kindle Direct Publishing (KDP): Empowering Authors to Share Their Stories

Kindle Direct Publishing (KDP) is a revolutionary platform that has transformed the world of publishing, making it accessible to authors of all backgrounds and genres. By providing a direct route to publish and distribute digital books, KDP has democratized the publishing industry and allowed authors to share their stories with a global audience. In this page, we will explore the world of Kindle Direct Publishing, its significance, how it works, responsibilities, challenges, and the potential compensation involved.

The Significance of Kindle Direct Publishing (KDP)

KDP holds immense significance in the world of publishing for several reasons:

Accessibility: KDP provides a platform for authors to publish their books easily, regardless of their location or prior publishing experience.

Global Reach: Authors can reach a global audience of millions of Kindle readers through Amazon's extensive distribution network.

Empowerment: KDP empowers authors to retain creative control and ownership of their work, allowing them to set pricing, make updates, and choose publishing formats.

Diverse Genres: KDP welcomes a diverse range of genres and writing styles, enabling authors to explore their unique storytelling voices.

How Kindle Direct Publishing (KDP) Works

Publishing a book on KDP involves the following steps:

Manuscript Preparation: Authors prepare their manuscript in a digital format, ensuring it meets KDP's formatting guidelines.

Book Upload: Authors create a KDP account, input book details, upload the manuscript, and design a book cover or use Amazon's cover creation tool.

Pricing and Distribution: Authors set the book's price, choose distribution options (e.g., Kindle, print-on-demand), and decide whether to enroll in Kindle Unlimited (KU) or Kindle Owners' Lending Library (KOLL).

Publishing: Authors click the "Publish" button, making their book available for sale on Amazon's Kindle Store.

Royalties: Authors earn royalties based on book sales and KU/KOLL borrows, with different royalty rates for different pricing options and distribution channels.

Responsibilities of KDP Authors

While KDP simplifies the publishing process, authors still have several responsibilities:

Quality Content: Ensuring their book is well-written, edited, and free of formatting errors.

Marketing: Promoting their book through social media, book signings, email marketing, and other promotional strategies.

Pricing and Strategy: Setting competitive prices and choosing effective pricing strategies.

Cover Design: Creating an eye-catching book cover that appeals to the target audience.

Managing Reviews: Encouraging readers to leave reviews and managing the book's online reputation.

Challenges in Kindle Direct Publishing (KDP)

Publishing on KDP presents its own set of challenges:

Competition: The Kindle Store is highly competitive, with millions of books available, making it challenging for new authors to gain visibility.

Marketing: Effective book marketing is essential but can be time-consuming and require additional skills.

Quality Control: Ensuring the manuscript is well-edited and free of errors is crucial for a positive reader experience.

Compensation in Kindle Direct Publishing (KDP)

The compensation in KDP varies widely based on factors such as book genre, pricing strategy, marketing efforts, and reader engagement. Authors can earn royalties ranging from 35% to 70% of the book's list price for Kindle eBooks, depending on the book's pricing and distribution choices.

Authors also have the opportunity to earn additional income through Kindle Unlimited (KU) and Kindle Owners' Lending Library (KOLL) borrows, which are paid based on a monthly global fund.

The potential income for KDP authors ranges from a few dollars to thousands or even millions annually, with top authors achieving significant success. However, it's important to note that many authors earn modest incomes, and success often requires persistence, marketing savvy, and writing skill.

Kindle Direct Publishing (KDP) has transformed the publishing landscape, offering authors a powerful platform to share their stories and ideas with the world. While challenges exist, those who excel in writing quality content, effective marketing, and reader engagement have the opportunity to build successful writing careers and potentially earn substantial income through their books. KDP empowers authors to become not just writers but publishers, bringing their creative visions to life and reaching readers on a global scale.

AIRBNB HOSTING

Airbnb Hosting: Opening Your Doors to a World of Travelers

Airbnb has revolutionized the way people travel and experience accommodations, offering a unique platform that allows individuals to open their homes to travelers from around the world. Hosting on Airbnb provides an opportunity to earn income, connect with diverse guests, and share the culture of your location. In this page, we'll explore the world of Airbnb hosting, its significance, how it works, responsibilities, challenges, and the potential compensation involved.

The Significance of Airbnb Hosting

Airbnb hosting is significant for several reasons:

Diverse Accommodations: It provides travelers with a wide range of accommodation options, from cozy apartments and unique cottages to luxurious villas and shared spaces.

Local Experiences: Airbnb hosts often offer insights into local culture, attractions, and traditions, enriching the traveler's experience.

Income Generation: Hosting offers a source of income for property owners, allowing them to leverage their assets.

Global Community: Airbnb creates a global community of hosts and guests, fostering connections and cultural exchanges.

How Airbnb Hosting Works

Becoming an Airbnb host involves the following steps:

Property Listing: Hosts create a listing for their property, including photos, descriptions, pricing, and availability.

Guest Bookings: Travelers search for listings, make bookings, and communicate with hosts through the Airbnb platform.

Check-In and Hosting: Hosts prepare their property, greet guests, provide information, and ensure a comfortable stay.

Guest Reviews: After the stay, both hosts and guests can leave reviews to build trust within the Airbnb community.

Payment: Hosts receive payment for bookings, with Airbnb handling transactions securely.

Responsibilities of Airbnb Hosts

While Airbnb simplifies the hosting process, hosts have various responsibilities:

Property Maintenance: Ensuring the property is clean, safe, and well-maintained for guests.

Communication: Promptly responding to inquiries, providing information, and addressing guest needs.

Pricing and Availability: Setting competitive prices, updating availability calendars, and adjusting rates for peak seasons.

Guest Experience: Creating a welcoming atmosphere, offering amenities, and providing local recommendations.

Legal Compliance: Adhering to local regulations, including tax requirements and rental permits.

Challenges in Airbnb Hosting

Hosting on Airbnb comes with its own set of challenges:

Guest Expectations: Meeting guest expectations and maintaining a high-quality experience can be demanding.

Property Management: Managing property upkeep, cleaning, and maintenance can be time-consuming.

Risk Management: Protecting against property damage, theft, or liability issues is essential.

Market Competition: The competitive nature of the platform may require hosts to continuously improve their listings and services.

Compensation in Airbnb Hosting

The compensation for Airbnb hosts varies widely based on factors such as location, property type, pricing strategy, and guest demand. Hosts earn income through guest bookings, with Airbnb taking a percentage of the booking amount as a service fee.

Potential earnings range from a few hundred to several thousand dollars per month for hosts with highly sought-after properties. Some hosts generate substantial income and even turn hosting into a full-time business. However, income can fluctuate depending on factors like occupancy rates and seasonal demand.

Airbnb hosting offers property owners an opportunity to earn income while sharing their homes and local culture with travelers. While challenges exist, successful hosts leverage their hospitality, property management skills, and market understanding to create positive guest experiences and generate income. Airbnb has redefined the travel industry, allowing people to explore the world while staying in unique and personalized accommodations offered by hosts who open their doors and hearts to guests from around the globe.

BLOGGING

Blogging: Crafting Words and Ideas into a Digital Journey

Blogging has become a powerful medium for individuals and businesses to share their thoughts, expertise, and stories with a global audience. Whether you're passionate about a specific topic or looking to establish an online presence, blogging offers an accessible platform to create, connect, and even earn income. In this page, we'll explore the world of blogging, its significance, how it works, responsibilities, challenges, and the potential compensation involved.

The Significance of Blogging

Blogging holds significance for various reasons:

Information Sharing: Blogs serve as valuable sources of information, offering insights, tips, and knowledge on a wide range of topics.

Community Building: Blogs foster communities of like-minded individuals, providing a platform for discussion and engagement.

Personal Expression: Blogging allows individuals to express their creativity, thoughts, and opinions in a personal and authentic way.

Business Growth: For businesses, blogs are effective tools for marketing, customer engagement, and brand building.

How Blogging Works

Creating and maintaining a blog involves several key steps:

Topic Selection: Bloggers choose a niche or topic they are passionate about or knowledgeable in.

Content Creation: Regularly publishing articles, posts, or multimedia content that resonate with the target audience.

Audience Engagement: Interacting with readers through comments, social media, and email newsletters.

Monetization: Exploring various methods to generate income, such as advertising, affiliate marketing, sponsored content, and product sales.

Responsibilities of Bloggers

While blogging offers flexibility, bloggers have several responsibilities:

Content Quality: Producing high-quality, informative, and engaging content that adds value to readers.

Consistency: Maintaining a regular posting schedule to keep readers engaged.

Audience Building: Actively growing and engaging with the blog's audience through various channels.

Monetization Strategies: Developing and implementing effective monetization strategies that align with the blog's niche and audience.

Challenges in Blogging

Blogging presents its own set of challenges:

Content Creation: Consistently generating fresh, valuable content can be time-consuming and creatively demanding.

Audience Growth: Building and retaining a dedicated readership can be challenging in a crowded online space.

Monetization: Earning substantial income through blogging may require time and a well-planned strategy.

Competition: The blogosphere is highly competitive, with millions of blogs vying for attention.

Compensation in Blogging

The compensation for bloggers varies widely based on factors such as niche, audience size, content quality, and monetization methods. Potential income streams for bloggers include:

Advertising: Earnings from display ads, sponsored posts, and affiliate marketing.

Affiliate Marketing: Earnings from promoting products or services and earning commissions on sales.

Sponsored Content: Payment for creating content sponsored by brands or companies.

Product Sales: Income generated from selling digital products, books, merchandise, or online courses.

Consulting and Services: Income from offering consulting services or expertise related to the blog's niche.

Successful bloggers can earn anywhere from a few hundred to several thousand dollars per month or even more. However, it may take time to build a substantial income, and not all bloggers achieve this level of success.

Blogging is a dynamic and versatile medium that offers individuals and businesses a platform to express themselves, share knowledge, and potentially generate income. While challenges exist, bloggers who excel in content creation, audience engagement, and monetization strategies can create a fulfilling online presence and, over time, build a successful and potentially lucrative blogging career. Blogging is not just about words; it's about connecting with an audience and taking them on a digital journey through the art of storytelling and information sharing.

SNEAKER FLIPPING

Sneaker Flipping: Turning Kicks into Profits in the World of Resale

Sneaker flipping, also known as sneaker reselling, has become a thriving subculture within the fashion and streetwear industry. It involves buying coveted sneakers and reselling them for a profit. This lucrative venture has attracted sneaker enthusiasts, entrepreneurs, and collectors alike. In this page, we'll delve into the world of sneaker flipping, its significance, how it works, responsibilities, challenges, and the potential compensation involved.

The Significance of Sneaker Flipping

Sneaker flipping is significant for various reasons:

Cultural Phenomenon: Sneakers have transcended their utilitarian purpose and become symbols of culture, fashion, and self-expression.

Exclusive Releases: Limited-edition and exclusive sneaker releases create hype and demand among collectors and enthusiasts.

Profit Potential: Sneaker flipping offers an opportunity for individuals to turn their passion for sneakers into a profitable business.

Market Dynamics: The sneaker resale market reflects broader trends in fashion, luxury, and consumer behavior.

How Sneaker Flipping Works

Sneaker flipping involves a multi-step process:

Product Knowledge: Flippers research and stay informed about upcoming sneaker releases, trends, and market values.

Purchase: They acquire sneakers through various means, including online releases, in-store purchases, or trading with other collectors.

Authentication: Ensuring the sneakers' authenticity is crucial to maintaining a reputable resale business.

Listing: Flippers list the sneakers for sale on online marketplaces, such as StockX, GOAT, eBay, or their own platforms.

Pricing: Setting prices based on market demand, rarity, condition, and trends.

Marketing: Promoting their listings through social media, sneaker forums, and online communities to attract potential buyers.

Shipping and Handling: Safely packaging and shipping sneakers to buyers.

Profit: Earning income from the price difference between the purchase and resale price.

Responsibilities of Sneaker Flippers

Successful sneaker flippers undertake various responsibilities:

Market Research: Staying informed about sneaker releases, trends, and market dynamics.

Financial Management: Budgeting for sneaker purchases and tracking expenses and profits.

Authentication: Developing expertise in identifying counterfeit sneakers to maintain trust among buyers.

Customer Service: Responding to inquiries, addressing buyer concerns, and handling returns or disputes.

Inventory Management: Tracking sneaker inventory, ensuring proper storage, and monitoring market values.

Challenges in Sneaker Flipping

Sneaker flipping is not without its challenges:

Competition: The sneaker resale market is highly competitive, with many flippers vying for the same sneakers.

Market Volatility: Market values can fluctuate, affecting the potential resale profit.

Authentication Risks: The risk of inadvertently purchasing counterfeit sneakers is a constant concern.

Initial Investment: Flippers often need a substantial initial investment to acquire sought-after sneakers.

Compensation in Sneaker Flipping

The compensation in sneaker flipping can vary significantly based on factors such as sneaker rarity, market demand, brand popularity, and the flipper's expertise. Successful flippers can earn profits ranging from a few hundred dollars to thousands of dollars per sneaker.

Some individuals have turned sneaker flipping into a full-time career and have generated substantial income. However, not all flippers achieve the same level of success, and profitability can fluctuate based on market conditions.

Sneaker flipping offers enthusiasts and entrepreneurs a unique opportunity to blend passion with profit. While it requires knowledge, dedication, and financial investment, the allure of acquiring and reselling coveted sneakers has turned this subculture into a thriving industry. For those who excel in sneaker flipping, it's not just about making money—it's about being part of a cultural phenomenon that celebrates self-expression, style, and the art of the sneaker.

DOG WALKING

Dog Walking: A Tail-Wagging Venture in Pet Care

Dog walking has become a popular and rewarding profession for animal lovers and entrepreneurs. This pet care service involves taking dogs for regular walks to provide exercise, socialization, and companionship. In this page, we'll explore the world of dog walking, its significance, how it works, responsibilities, challenges, and the potential compensation involved.

The Significance of Dog Walking

Dog walking is significant for several reasons:

Pet Health: Regular walks help dogs maintain physical health, reduce obesity, and provide mental stimulation.

Pet Socialization: Walks allow dogs to interact with other dogs, people, and the environment, improving their social skills.

Owner Convenience: Dog owners often rely on professional dog walkers to ensure their pets receive regular exercise, especially when they have busy schedules.

Job Creation: Dog walking creates job opportunities for animal enthusiasts and individuals looking for flexible work.

How Dog Walking Works

Dog walking involves the following steps:

Client Acquisition: Dog walkers market their services through various channels, such as online platforms, social media, or local advertising.

Initial Consultation: Meeting with potential clients to discuss their dog's needs, behavior, and any specific instructions.

Walking Schedule: Determining the frequency and duration of walks based on the dog's age, breed, and energy level.

Walking Sessions: Walking dogs on agreed-upon routes, ensuring they receive exercise and bathroom breaks.

Safety and Care: Monitoring the dog's well-being, keeping them safe from hazards, and cleaning up after them.

Client Communication: Providing feedback to clients about the dog's behavior and overall well-being during walks.

Responsibilities of Dog Walkers

Dog walkers have several responsibilities:

Pet Safety: Ensuring the safety of the dogs during walks, including leash control and awareness of potential hazards.

Reliability: Sticking to scheduled walk times and informing clients of any changes or delays.

Physical Fitness: Being physically fit and capable of handling dogs of various sizes and energy levels.

Emergency Preparedness: Knowing how to respond to emergencies, including injuries or lost dogs.

Professionalism: Maintaining a professional demeanor and treating clients' pets with care and respect.

Challenges in Dog Walking

Dog walking presents its own set of challenges:

Weather Conditions: Walkers must be prepared to work in various weather conditions, including rain, snow, or extreme heat.

Pet Behavior: Handling dogs with diverse personalities and behavior traits can be challenging.

Client Expectations: Meeting client expectations and accommodating individual dog needs.

Competition: The dog walking industry can be competitive, with multiple service providers in many areas.

Compensation in Dog Walking

The compensation for dog walkers can vary based on factors such as location, the number of clients, the duration of walks, and additional services offered. Typically, dog walkers charge clients on a per-walk basis, with rates ranging from $10 to $30 or more per walk, depending on the region and services provided.

Full-time professional dog walkers who build a sizable client base can potentially earn a substantial income. Additionally, walkers may receive tips from satisfied clients as a bonus to their base fees.

Dog walking is a fulfilling profession that allows individuals to combine their love for animals with a flexible and rewarding career. While it requires physical fitness, patience, and a love for dogs, the opportunity to provide exercise and companionship to furry companions can be highly satisfying. As more dog owners seek the services of professional dog walkers, this industry continues to grow, offering a viable career path for those passionate about pets.

HOUSE FLIPPING

Flipping Houses: Transforming Real Estate into Profits

Flipping houses has gained popularity as a lucrative venture in the real estate industry. It involves purchasing distressed or undervalued properties, renovating them, and then selling them for a profit. Successful house flippers can generate substantial income, but the process requires careful planning, renovation expertise, and market knowledge. In this page, we'll delve into the world of house flipping, its significance, how it works, responsibilities, challenges, and the potential compensation involved.

The Significance of House Flipping

House flipping is significant for several reasons:

Property Revitalization: Flippers often breathe new life into neglected properties, improving neighborhoods and increasing property values.

Investment Opportunities: It provides a means for real estate investors to generate significant returns on their investments.

Housing Market Impact: Flipping activity can influence the overall real estate market by driving demand for construction materials and labor.

Job Creation: Renovation projects create jobs for contractors, construction workers, and tradespeople.

How House Flipping Works

Flipping houses involves a multi-step process:

Property Acquisition: Flippers identify suitable properties through various means, including auctions, real estate listings, or distressed property leads.

Market Analysis: They assess the potential for profit by evaluating the property's location, condition, and market trends.

Purchase and Financing: Flippers secure financing, purchase the property, and often allocate a budget for renovations.

Renovation: The property undergoes extensive renovations and upgrades to increase its market value.

Listing and Sale: Once the renovations are complete, the property is listed for sale at an increased price.

Profit: Flippers earn income from the difference between the purchase, renovation, and sale prices, minus expenses.

Responsibilities of House Flippers

Successful house flippers take on various responsibilities:

Property Assessment: Identifying properties with profit potential and conducting thorough inspections.

Renovation Management: Overseeing renovation projects, including budgeting, hiring contractors, and ensuring quality work.

Market Knowledge: Staying informed about local real estate market trends, values, and demand.

Financial Management: Managing budgets, tracking expenses, and maximizing cost-efficiency.

Legal Compliance: Adhering to local building codes, permits, and zoning regulations.

Challenges in House Flipping

House flipping presents several challenges:

Financial Risks: Flippers invest significant capital upfront, and market fluctuations can impact profitability.

Renovation Delays: Delays in renovation projects can lead to increased costs and lost potential income.

Market Saturation: High competition in certain markets can make it difficult to find suitable properties.

Market Downturns: Economic downturns or shifts in the real estate market can affect property values and demand.

Compensation in House Flipping

The compensation in house flipping varies based on factors such as location, property type, renovation costs, and market conditions. Successful flippers can earn substantial profits, with potential returns ranging from thousands to hundreds of thousands of dollars per property.

The average profit margin for house flippers is typically around 10% to 20% of the property's after-repair value (ARV). However, some flips can yield even higher returns, while others may result in losses.

House flipping offers individuals and investors an opportunity to generate income by revitalizing properties and capitalizing on real estate market trends. While it requires significant financial investment, renovation expertise, and market knowledge, the potential for substantial profits makes it an appealing venture. Successful house flippers leverage their skills and understanding of the real estate market to transform distressed properties into profitable investments, contributing to the revitalization and growth of neighborhoods and communities.

WEBSITE FLIPPING

Website Flipping: Navigating the Digital Real Estate Marketplace

Website flipping is a dynamic online business model that involves acquiring, improving, and selling websites for profit. It has gained popularity as an attractive venture for entrepreneurs and investors looking to capitalize on the digital real estate market. In this page, we'll explore the world of website flipping, its significance, how it works, responsibilities, challenges, and the potential compensation involved.

The Significance of Website Flipping

Website flipping holds significance for several reasons:

Digital Real Estate: Websites are valuable digital properties with the potential to generate income through various online monetization methods.

Entrepreneurship: It provides a platform for entrepreneurs to start, grow, and sell online businesses.

Income Diversification: Website flipping allows individuals to diversify their income streams and explore new niches and markets.

Market Trends: The digital landscape is ever-evolving, creating opportunities for those who can identify and leverage emerging trends.

How Website Flipping Works

Website flipping involves a multi-step process:

Website Acquisition: Flippers identify websites with profit potential through various channels, such as online marketplaces, auctions, or direct sales.

Due Diligence: Thoroughly researching and evaluating the website, including its traffic, revenue, content quality, and market niche.

Purchase and Transition: Acquiring the website, making necessary improvements, and transitioning ownership.

Monetization Optimization: Enhancing the website's revenue streams through improved marketing, SEO, content, and user experience.

Listing and Sale: When the website's value has increased, it's listed for sale in online marketplaces or through broker services.

Profit: Flippers earn income from the difference between the purchase and sale prices, minus expenses and improvements.

Responsibilities of Website Flippers

Successful website flippers take on various responsibilities:

Market Research: Identifying trends, niches, and websites with profit potential.

Due Diligence: Conducting thorough website evaluations and negotiations.

Improvements: Managing and implementing necessary enhancements, including content quality, design, and monetization strategies.

Marketing: Promoting and growing the website's audience and revenue.

Financial Management: Tracking expenses, budgets, and revenue to maximize profitability.

Challenges in Website Flipping

Website flipping presents its own set of challenges:

Market Volatility: The digital landscape can be unpredictable, with rapid shifts in user behavior, search engine algorithms, and market trends.

Monetization Risks: Websites may rely on monetization methods that can be affected by market conditions or algorithm changes.

Content Quality: Maintaining or improving the quality of website content can be time-consuming and resource-intensive.

Competition: The online marketplace for websites is competitive, with many buyers and sellers vying for attractive opportunities.

Compensation in Website Flipping

The compensation in website flipping varies widely based on factors such as website niche, traffic, revenue, and improvements made. Profit margins can range from a few hundred dollars to hundreds of thousands of dollars per transaction.

Typically, successful website flippers aim for profit margins of 30% or more, although this can vary depending on the website's potential and the level of risk involved.

Website flipping offers individuals and entrepreneurs an exciting opportunity to enter the digital real estate market, acquire online properties, and generate income through strategic improvements and resale. While it requires a keen understanding of online trends, digital marketing, and website management, the potential for significant profits makes it a compelling venture. Successful website flippers leverage their skills and insights to identify, enhance, and sell online businesses, contributing to the dynamic landscape of the internet.

DOG BREEDING

Dog Breeding is it for you!

Dog breeding is a passionate pursuit for many, involving the careful selection, pairing, and raising of dogs to produce healthy and desirable offspring. Beyond the joy of working with these beloved animals, it can also serve as a source of income for those committed to responsible breeding practices. In this page, we'll explore the world of dog breeding, its significance, how it works, responsibilities, challenges, and the potential compensation involved.

The Significance of Dog Breeding

Dog breeding holds significance for several reasons:

Preservation of Breeds: Responsible breeders play a vital role in preserving and improving specific dog breeds, maintaining their unique traits and characteristics.

Healthy Companions: Ethical breeders prioritize the health and well-being of dogs, ensuring that puppies are raised in nurturing environments.

Meeting Demand: As people seek specific breeds or traits in their canine companions, breeders fulfill the demand for well-bred puppies.

Income Opportunity: For dedicated breeders, dog breeding can become a business that generates income through puppy sales.

How Dog Breeding Works

Dog breeding involves a careful and selective process:

Breed Selection: Breeders choose specific breeds based on their knowledge, experience, and market demand.

Pairing: Selecting compatible male and female dogs with desirable traits, health records, and lineage.

Mating: Allowing the selected dogs to mate naturally or through artificial insemination, ensuring successful breeding.

Pregnancy and Whelping: Caring for the pregnant mother, providing proper nutrition and veterinary care, and preparing for the birth of puppies.

Puppy Care: Raising puppies with love, socializing them, and ensuring their health and well-being.

Marketing and Sales: Finding suitable homes for puppies through marketing, advertising, and screening potential buyers.

Responsibilities of Dog Breeders

Responsible dog breeders undertake various responsibilities:

Health Screening: Conducting health screenings and genetic testing to minimize hereditary health issues in the breed.

Breeding Ethics: Following ethical breeding practices, which include not overbreeding, providing proper care, and avoiding inbreeding.

Puppy Placement: Ensuring puppies are placed in loving and responsible homes, often through a comprehensive screening process.

Record Keeping: Maintaining accurate records of breeding, health, and lineage to track and improve bloodlines.

Continued Learning: Staying informed about the latest breeding practices, health advancements, and breed standards.

Challenges in Dog Breeding

Dog breeding presents its own set of challenges:

Health Risks: Breeding can involve health risks for both the mother and puppies, including complications during pregnancy and birth.

Ethical Considerations: Maintaining ethical breeding standards and avoiding practices that harm dogs or result in overpopulation.

Market Competition: The dog breeding market can be competitive, especially for popular breeds.

Regulatory Compliance: Complying with local, state, and national regulations related to breeding and animal welfare.

Compensation in Dog Breeding

The compensation in dog breeding varies significantly based on factors such as breed popularity, the breeder's reputation, health testing, and the quality of puppies produced. Puppies from well-bred and healthy bloodlines can command higher prices.

Dog breeders can earn income ranging from a few hundred to several thousand dollars per puppy. Successful breeders with in-demand breeds and excellent reputations may generate substantial income. However, it's important to consider the expenses related to breeding, including health care, food, and marketing.

Dog breeding offers individuals an opportunity to combine their love for dogs with a potential source of income. Responsible breeders prioritize the health, well-being, and ethics of breeding, ensuring that puppies are raised in loving environments. While challenges exist, dedicated breeders who adhere to ethical standards can find fulfillment in contributing to the well-being of dogs and providing families with cherished canine companions. Dog breeding is not just a business—it's a passion that celebrates the beauty, diversity, and unique qualities of our canine friends.

FLIPPING CARS

Flipping Cars: Driving Profits in the Auto Resale Market

Car flipping, often referred to as automotive flipping, is a dynamic venture that involves buying used cars, refurbishing them, and reselling them for a profit. This practice has gained popularity among auto enthusiasts, entrepreneurs, and those with a knack for automotive mechanics. In this page, we'll explore the world of car flipping, its significance, how it works, responsibilities, challenges, and the potential compensation involved.

The Significance of Car Flipping

Car flipping is significant for several reasons:

Vehicle Resale: It provides a valuable service by refurbishing and improving used cars, making them accessible to buyers seeking affordable and reliable transportation.

Investment Opportunity: Car flipping allows individuals to invest in vehicles, improve their condition, and sell them at a profit.

Market Dynamics: It reflects broader trends in the automotive market, including consumer demand for specific makes and models.

Economic Impact: Automotive flipping contributes to economic activity by supporting the automotive aftermarket industry and creating jobs for mechanics and refurbishment specialists.

How Car Flipping Works

Car flipping involves a series of steps:

Vehicle Sourcing: Flippers find suitable cars for purchase through various channels, such as auctions, private sales, or online listings.

Assessment: Thoroughly evaluating the car's condition, identifying necessary repairs, and estimating refurbishment costs.

Purchase and Repairs: Acquiring the vehicle and performing the required repairs, which may include mechanical, cosmetic, and safety improvements.

Detailing and Maintenance: Ensuring the car is in top-notch condition, including detailing, maintenance, and any required safety inspections.

Pricing: Determining a competitive selling price based on market trends, the car's condition, and any upgrades or improvements.

Marketing and Sale: Listing the car for sale through online platforms, advertisements, or local listings.

Profit: Earning income from the difference between the purchase and sale prices, minus expenses and refurbishment costs.

Responsibilities of Car Flippers

Successful car flippers take on various responsibilities:

Vehicle Knowledge: Maintaining knowledge about different makes, models, and market trends.

Mechanical Skills: Having or hiring mechanical expertise to perform necessary repairs and maintenance.

Budgeting and Financial Management: Managing budgets, tracking expenses, and estimating potential profits.

Market Research: Staying informed about the local and regional used car market, pricing trends, and consumer preferences.

Challenges in Car Flipping

Car flipping presents its own set of challenges:

Market Fluctuations: The used car market can be influenced by factors like economic conditions and shifts in consumer preferences.

Mechanical Risks: Unexpected mechanical issues or repair costs can impact profitability.

Regulatory Compliance: Complying with local regulations, including safety inspections and emissions standards.

Competition: The automotive resale market can be highly competitive, with many sellers vying for the same buyers.

Compensation in Car Flipping

The compensation in car flipping varies widely based on factors such as the initial purchase price, refurbishment costs, market demand, and the selling price. Successful flippers can earn profits ranging from a few hundred to several thousand dollars per vehicle.

Profits are influenced by the car's make and model, its condition, and the quality of refurbishments and improvements. Flippers with expertise in identifying undervalued cars, efficient repair processes, and effective marketing strategies can maximize their earnings.

Car flipping offers individuals an opportunity to combine their passion for automobiles with a potential source of income. While it requires knowledge of the automotive market, mechanical skills, and financial acumen, the potential for profit makes it an appealing venture. Successful car flippers take pride in their ability to rejuvenate and improve vehicles, providing buyers with reliable transportation options and contributing to the dynamic world of automotive resale. Car flipping is not just about buying and selling—it's about transforming vehicles into valuable assets and driving profits in the process.

PRESSURE WASHING
BUSINESS

Pressure Washing Business: Cleaning Up and Profiting In Style

A pressure washing business is a dynamic and rewarding venture that involves using high-pressure water to clean and restore surfaces. Whether it's reviving a grimy sidewalk, washing a house exterior, or revitalizing a commercial property, pressure washing services are in demand. In this page, we'll explore the world of pressure washing, its significance, how it works, responsibilities, challenges, and the potential compensation involved.

The Significance of Pressure Washing

Pressure washing holds significance for various reasons:

Cleanliness: It helps maintain and restore the appearance of surfaces, enhancing curb appeal and hygiene.

Property Maintenance: Regular pressure washing can extend the life of buildings, decks, driveways, and other structures.

Environmental Benefits: Using high-pressure water reduces the need for harsh chemicals in cleaning, making it an eco-friendly option.

Business Opportunities: Starting a pressure washing business provides opportunities for entrepreneurs and individuals looking for flexible work.

How a Pressure Washing Business Works

Operating a pressure washing business involves a series of steps:

Equipment and Supplies: Acquiring the necessary pressure washing equipment, safety gear, and cleaning solutions.

Client Acquisition: Marketing and advertising services to attract residential and commercial clients.

Assessment and Quoting: Inspecting the area to be cleaned, providing quotes, and scheduling appointments.

Cleaning Process: Using high-pressure water equipment to clean surfaces, remove dirt, mold, mildew, and stains.

Safety: Ensuring safety for both workers and the property being cleaned.

Billing and Payments: Handling invoices, payments, and record-keeping.

Customer Satisfaction: Building a reputation for quality work and client satisfaction.

Responsibilities of a Pressure Washing Business Owner

Successful pressure washing business owners undertake various responsibilities:

Technical Expertise: Becoming proficient in pressure washing techniques and equipment operation.

Client Communication: Establishing clear communication with clients, understanding their needs, and providing accurate quotes.

Safety Compliance: Ensuring safety protocols are followed to prevent accidents or property damage.

Marketing and Promotion: Implementing marketing strategies to attract and retain clients.

Equipment Maintenance: Maintaining pressure washing equipment in good working condition.

Challenges in the Pressure Washing Business

Running a pressure washing business comes with its own set of challenges:

Seasonal Variations: The demand for pressure washing services can be seasonal, depending on weather conditions.

Competition: The market can be competitive, with many service providers vying for clients.

Equipment Costs: Pressure washing equipment can be a significant upfront investment.

Safety Risks: Working with high-pressure water can be hazardous if not done correctly.

Compensation in the Pressure Washing Business

The compensation in a pressure washing business varies based on factors such as location, market demand, services offered, and pricing strategies. Pressure washing businesses typically charge clients on a per-project or hourly basis.

Profits can range from a few hundred to several thousand dollars per project. Successful pressure washing business owners can generate substantial income, especially when they offer specialized services or cater to a niche market.

A pressure washing business provides individuals with an opportunity to combine their love for cleanliness and outdoor work with a potential source of income. While it requires technical expertise, marketing skills, and investment in equipment, the satisfaction of transforming dirty surfaces into clean, vibrant ones can be highly rewarding. Pressure washing is not just about water and equipment; it's about revitalizing spaces, enhancing property value, and delivering exceptional service to clients who appreciate the difference a thorough clean can make.

MEDICAL SUPPLY DELIVERY

Delivery of Medical Supplies: Bringing Care to Your Doorstep

The delivery of medical supplies is a crucial and compassionate service that plays a vital role in the healthcare industry. It involves the transportation of essential medical equipment, medications, and supplies to healthcare facilities, patients' homes, and healthcare providers. This service ensures that healthcare professionals can provide quality care, and patients can receive the essential supplies they need. In this page, we'll explore the world of medical supply delivery, its significance, how it works, responsibilities, challenges, and the potential compensation involved.

The Significance of Medical Supply Delivery

Medical supply delivery is significant for several reasons:

Patient Care: It enables patients to access necessary medical equipment and supplies without leaving their homes, improving their quality of life and health outcomes.

Healthcare Operations: Healthcare facilities rely on timely deliveries of medical supplies to maintain operations and provide appropriate care to patients.

Emergency Response: Medical supply delivery plays a vital role in disaster response and emergency situations, ensuring that essential supplies are available when needed most.

Logistical Support: It supports the healthcare supply chain, helping hospitals and clinics manage their inventory efficiently.

How Medical Supply Delivery Works

Operating a medical supply delivery service involves a series of steps:

Supplier Collaboration: Establishing partnerships with medical supply manufacturers, pharmacies, hospitals, and healthcare facilities.

Order Processing: Receiving orders for medical supplies from healthcare providers, patients, or caregivers.

Inventory Management: Maintaining a well-organized inventory of medical supplies, including durable medical equipment (DME), medications, and disposables.

Routing and Scheduling: Planning efficient routes for delivery and scheduling deliveries based on urgency and patient needs.

Transportation: Using appropriate vehicles to transport medical supplies safely, ensuring compliance with regulations for the transportation of hazardous materials when necessary.

Documentation: Keeping accurate records of deliveries, including patient information, signatures, and inventory tracking.

Communication: Maintaining clear and timely communication with healthcare providers, patients, and caregivers.

Responsibilities of Medical Supply Delivery Personnel

Those involved in medical supply delivery have various responsibilities:

Logistics: Managing the logistics of the delivery process, including route planning and scheduling.

Patient Interaction: Providing a high level of customer service and compassion when interacting with patients or caregivers.

Compliance: Ensuring compliance with regulations related to the transportation and delivery of medical supplies.

Safety: Prioritizing safety measures to protect both delivery personnel and patients.

Efficiency: Streamlining delivery processes to meet delivery timeframes.

Challenges in Medical Supply Delivery

Medical supply delivery comes with its own set of challenges:

Patient Privacy: Handling sensitive medical information and respecting patient privacy.

Safety Concerns: Safely transporting medications and hazardous materials when required.

Delivery Delays: Addressing unexpected delays or logistical challenges.

Regulatory Compliance: Navigating complex regulations, especially when delivering controlled substances or specialized medical supplies.

Compensation in Medical Supply Delivery

The compensation in medical supply delivery varies depending on factors such as the size and scope of the operation, geographic location, and the level of responsibility. Delivery personnel may be compensated on an hourly basis or receive a salary.

Hourly wages for medical supply delivery personnel typically range from $12 to $25 or more per hour, depending on factors like experience, responsibilities, and the complexity of the deliveries.

Medical supply delivery is a vital and compassionate service that ensures patients receive the essential healthcare supplies they need, where and when they need them. Those involved in this field play a critical role in the healthcare ecosystem, supporting patients, healthcare providers, and healthcare facilities. While it involves logistical challenges and regulatory considerations, the reward comes from knowing that your efforts directly contribute to the well-being and care of individuals in need.

FOREX TRADING

Forex Trading: Navigating the Global Currency Markets

Forex (foreign exchange) trading is a dynamic and potentially lucrative venture that involves the buying and selling of currencies in the global financial markets. Traders speculate on currency price movements, aiming to profit from fluctuations in exchange rates. In this page, we'll explore the world of forex trading, its significance, how it works, responsibilities, challenges, and the potential compensation involved.

The Significance of Forex Trading

Forex trading holds significance for several reasons:

Global Finance: It's the largest financial market in the world, with a daily trading volume exceeding $6 trillion, making it a key player in the global financial system.

Currency Exchange: Forex trading facilitates international trade by providing a means to exchange one currency for another.

Investment Opportunity: Individuals and institutions can participate in forex trading to diversify their investment portfolios and potentially generate returns.

Market Liquidity: The forex market's high liquidity ensures that traders can enter and exit positions quickly.

How Forex Trading Works

Forex trading involves several key components:

Currency Pairs: Traders select currency pairs, such as EUR/USD (Euro/US Dollar), to speculate on. They decide whether the base currency (the first in the pair) will strengthen or weaken relative to the quote currency (the second in the pair).

Broker Selection: Traders choose a forex broker to access the market. Brokers provide trading platforms, leverage, and access to currency pairs.

Technical and Fundamental Analysis: Traders use technical analysis (chart patterns, indicators) and fundamental analysis (economic news, geopolitical events) to make informed trading decisions.

Orders and Positions: Traders place orders to buy or sell currency pairs at specific price levels. They can open long (buy) or short (sell) positions.

Risk Management: Implementing risk management strategies, such as setting stop-loss and take-profit orders, to mitigate potential losses.

Leverage: Traders may use leverage, provided by brokers, to control larger positions with a smaller amount of capital. While it magnifies profits, it also increases the risk of losses.

Responsibilities of Forex Traders

Forex traders have various responsibilities:

Market Analysis: Staying informed about market conditions, news events, and currency pair dynamics.

Risk Management: Managing risk through position sizing, stop-loss orders, and risk-reward ratios.

Continuous Learning: Adapting to evolving market conditions and refining trading strategies.

Emotional Discipline: Maintaining emotional discipline to avoid impulsive decisions driven by fear or greed.

Challenges in Forex Trading

Forex trading presents its own set of challenges:

Risk of Loss: Trading carries a high risk of financial loss, especially when traders lack experience or effective risk management strategies.

Market Volatility: Currency markets can be highly volatile, with price fluctuations driven by economic data releases and geopolitical events.

Information Overload: Traders must sift through a vast amount of information and news to make informed decisions.

Psychological Pressure: Maintaining emotional discipline and managing psychological stress is crucial for success.

Compensation in Forex Trading

The compensation in forex trading varies widely based on factors such as trading strategy, risk tolerance, and capital investment. Traders can earn profits or incur losses, and there is no fixed salary or hourly wage.

Successful forex traders can potentially generate substantial income, with returns ranging from a few percent to several hundred percent of their invested capital in a year. However, it's important to note that not all traders are profitable, and many traders experience losses.

Forex trading offers individuals and institutions a dynamic and accessible avenue for participating in the global financial markets. While it holds the potential for significant profits, it also carries inherent risks. Success in forex trading requires a solid understanding of market dynamics, technical and fundamental analysis, risk management, and emotional discipline. Traders who are well-prepared and continuously educate themselves can potentially navigate the complexities of the forex market and strive for financial success.

CLEANING BUSINESS

Starting a Cleaning Business: Transforming Mess into Success

Starting a cleaning business can be a fulfilling entrepreneurial endeavor, offering the opportunity to create a successful venture while providing valuable cleaning services to residential and commercial clients. In this page, we'll explore the world of starting a cleaning business, its significance, how it works, responsibilities, challenges, and the potential compensation involved.

The Significance of Starting a Cleaning Business

Starting a cleaning business holds significance for several reasons:

Cleaner Living and Workspaces: Cleaning services contribute to healthier, more pleasant living and working environments, improving quality of life and productivity.

Time Savings: Busy individuals and businesses rely on cleaning services to save time and delegate cleaning tasks.

Business Opportunities: Entrepreneurial individuals can start and grow cleaning businesses, capitalizing on a steady demand for cleaning services.

Job Creation: Cleaning businesses create job opportunities for individuals in the cleaning industry.

How Starting a Cleaning Business Works

Starting a cleaning business involves several key steps:

Business Planning: Develop a comprehensive business plan that outlines your target market, services offered, pricing strategies, and marketing plan.

Legal Considerations: Register your business, obtain necessary licenses, and secure insurance coverage to protect your business and clients.

Equipment and Supplies: Invest in cleaning equipment, cleaning supplies, and safety gear for your cleaning team.

Marketing and Advertising: Promote your cleaning business through online platforms, local advertising, and networking.

Client Acquisition: Attract clients through marketing efforts and referrals, both residential and commercial.

Cleaning Services: Deliver high-quality cleaning services, meeting or exceeding client expectations.

Customer Satisfaction: Build a reputation for reliability, professionalism, and excellent customer service.

Responsibilities of Cleaning Business Owners

Starting a cleaning business comes with various responsibilities:

Client Communication: Establishing effective communication with clients, understanding their cleaning needs, and providing quotes.

Staff Management: If you hire cleaning staff, manage their schedules, training, and performance.

Quality Control: Ensuring consistent quality in your cleaning services to retain clients.

Scheduling: Efficiently schedule cleaning appointments and manage staff schedules.

Financial Management: Handle billing, invoicing, and financial records.

Challenges in Starting a Cleaning Business

Starting a cleaning business presents its own set of challenges:

Competition: The cleaning industry can be competitive, with many businesses vying for clients.

Labor and Staffing: Recruiting and retaining reliable cleaning staff can be challenging.

Client Trust: Building trust with clients is essential for success, especially for residential clients entering their homes.

Scaling: Expanding the business while maintaining quality can be a challenge.

Compensation in the Cleaning Business

The compensation in the cleaning business varies based on factors such as location, services offered, pricing structure, and the number of clients. Cleaning businesses often charge clients based on the size of the area to be cleaned or an hourly rate.

Cleaning businesses can earn profits ranging from a few hundred to several thousand dollars per month. The income potential depends on factors such as the number of clients, the scope of services, and the pricing strategy.

Starting a cleaning business is a rewarding way to enter the entrepreneurial world while providing valuable services to clients. While it requires dedication, planning, and hard work, the potential for growth and success is substantial. Cleaning business owners have the opportunity to transform messy spaces into pristine environments, improve the lives of their clients, and create a thriving business in the process.

MOBILE LOCKSMITH

Starting a Mobile Locksmith Business: Unlocking Entrepreneurial Success

Starting a mobile locksmith business is an entrepreneurial venture that offers the opportunity to provide valuable locksmith services while building a profitable business. As a mobile locksmith, you'll offer on-the-go lock and key solutions to residential and commercial clients. In this page, we'll explore the world of starting a mobile locksmith business, its significance, how it works, responsibilities, challenges, and the potential compensation involved.

The Significance of Starting a Mobile Locksmith Business

Starting a mobile locksmith business holds significance for several reasons:

Security: Locksmith services play a critical role in ensuring the security and safety of homes, businesses, and vehicles.

Convenience: Mobile locksmiths offer convenience by providing services at clients' locations, saving them time and effort.

Emergency Assistance: Mobile locksmiths are often called upon in emergencies, such as lockouts, making their services indispensable.

Business Opportunities: Entrepreneurial individuals can establish and grow locksmith businesses, serving a broad range of clients.

How Starting a Mobile Locksmith Business Works

Starting a mobile locksmith business involves several key steps:

Business Planning: Develop a business plan outlining your target market, services offered, pricing structure, and marketing strategies.

Legal Requirements: Register your business, obtain the necessary licenses, and ensure compliance with local regulations.

Equipment and Tools: Invest in locksmith tools, equipment, and a well-equipped mobile service vehicle.

Marketing and Promotion: Promote your mobile locksmith business through online platforms, local advertising, and networking.

Client Acquisition: Attract clients through marketing efforts, referrals, and online presence.

Service Delivery: Offer a range of locksmith services, including lockouts, rekeying, lock repairs, and key duplication, while providing exceptional customer service.

Emergency Response: Be prepared to provide emergency locksmith services 24/7, as lockouts and security issues can occur at any time.

Responsibilities of Mobile Locksmith Business Owners

Mobile locksmith business owners have various responsibilities:

Client Communication: Establishing effective communication with clients, understanding their locksmith needs, and providing accurate quotes.

Technician Training: If you hire locksmith technicians, ensure they are trained, skilled, and licensed to perform locksmith services.

Service Quality: Maintaining high service quality and reliability to build trust and client loyalty.

Scheduling: Efficiently schedule service appointments and manage the availability of mobile locksmith services.

Financial Management: Handle billing, invoicing, and financial records.

Challenges in Starting a Mobile Locksmith Business

Starting a mobile locksmith business presents its own set of challenges:

Competition: The locksmith industry can be competitive, with many local locksmiths and larger franchises.

Emergency Response: Being available for 24/7 emergency service can be demanding.

Security Concerns: Dealing with security-related issues requires utmost professionalism and ethics.

Skills and Training: Ensuring that you and your technicians are adequately trained and knowledgeable in locksmithing.

Compensation in the Mobile Locksmith Business

The compensation in a mobile locksmith business varies based on factors such as location, services offered, pricing structure, and the number of clients served. Locksmiths often charge clients based on the specific service provided.

Profits can range from a few hundred to several thousand dollars per month, depending on factors such as the number of service calls, the scope of services offered, and pricing strategies.

Starting a mobile locksmith business is a practical and potentially profitable venture that allows you to provide essential locksmith services while building a business. While it requires training, equipment investment, and dedication to quality service, the potential for growth and success is significant. Mobile locksmiths play a critical role in enhancing security and assisting clients in lockout situations, making their services invaluable to communities and businesses.

YARD MAINTENANCE BUSINESS

Starting a Landscaping or Yard Maintenance Business: Cultivating Green Success

Starting a landscaping or yard maintenance business is a rewarding entrepreneurial endeavor that allows you to transform outdoor spaces while creating a sustainable and profitable venture. These businesses offer a range of services, from lawn care to landscape design, and cater to both residential and commercial clients. In this page, we'll explore the world of starting a landscaping or yard maintenance business, its significance, how it works, responsibilities, challenges, and the potential compensation involved.

The Significance of Starting a Landscaping or Yard Maintenance Business

Starting a landscaping or yard maintenance business holds significance for several reasons:

Enhanced Beauty: Landscaping services improve the aesthetics of homes, businesses, and public spaces, enhancing their curb appeal.

Environmental Impact: Landscapers contribute to environmental sustainability by maintaining healthy green spaces and promoting responsible landscaping practices.

Property Value: Well-maintained landscapes can significantly increase property values.

Business Opportunities: Entrepreneurs can establish and grow landscaping businesses, serving a diverse clientele.

How Starting a Landscaping or Yard Maintenance Business Works

Starting a landscaping or yard maintenance business involves several key steps:

Business Planning: Develop a comprehensive business plan outlining your target market, services offered, pricing structure, and marketing strategies.

Legal Considerations: Register your business, obtain necessary licenses, and secure insurance coverage for liability protection.

Equipment and Tools: Invest in landscaping equipment, including lawnmowers, trimmers, and gardening tools, as well as a reliable work vehicle.

Marketing and Promotion: Promote your landscaping business through online platforms, local advertising, and networking.

Client Acquisition: Attract clients through marketing efforts, referrals, and a well-designed portfolio showcasing your previous work.

Service Delivery: Offer a range of landscaping services, such as lawn care, planting, landscaping, and maintenance, while providing excellent customer service.

Responsibilities of Landscaping or Yard Maintenance Business Owners

Owners of landscaping or yard maintenance businesses have various responsibilities:

Client Communication: Establish effective communication with clients, understand their landscaping needs, and provide accurate quotes.

Team Management: If you hire landscaping crews, manage their schedules, training, and performance.

Service Quality: Maintain high-quality service standards to build trust and loyalty with clients.

Project Management: Efficiently schedule and manage landscaping projects to meet client expectations.

Financial Management: Handle billing, invoicing, and financial records.

Challenges in Starting a Landscaping or Yard Maintenance Business

Starting a landscaping or yard maintenance business presents its own set of challenges:

Seasonal Variations: The demand for landscaping services can be seasonal, depending on climate and location.

Competition: The landscaping industry can be competitive, with many local providers.

Labor and Staffing: Recruiting and retaining skilled landscaping staff can be challenging.

Market Trends: Staying up-to-date with landscaping trends and eco-friendly practices is essential.

Compensation in Landscaping or Yard Maintenance Business

The compensation in a landscaping or yard maintenance business varies based on factors such as location, services offered, pricing structure, and the number of clients served. Landscapers often charge clients based on the scope and complexity of the project.

Profits can range from a few hundred to several thousand dollars per month, depending on factors such as the number of projects, size of contracts, and pricing strategies.

Starting a landscaping or yard maintenance business is a fulfilling way to create a thriving venture while enhancing outdoor spaces for clients. While it requires investment in equipment, training, and marketing efforts, the potential for growth and success is significant. Landscaping businesses not only transform landscapes but also contribute to the beauty and sustainability of communities, making their services invaluable to homeowners and businesses alike.

SUBSCRIPTION BOX SERVICE

Starting a Subscription Box Service: Unboxing Entrepreneurial Success

Starting a subscription box service is an exciting and innovative entrepreneurial venture that allows you to curate and deliver unique products and experiences to subscribers on a regular basis. Subscription boxes have gained immense popularity in recent years, offering a wide range of products, from gourmet foods to beauty products and books. In this page, we'll explore the world of starting a subscription box service, its significance, how it works, responsibilities, challenges, and the potential compensation involved.

The Significance of Starting a Subscription Box Service

Starting a subscription box service holds significance for several reasons:

Consumer Convenience: Subscription boxes offer consumers a convenient way to discover and enjoy new products without leaving their homes.

Personalization: Subscription box services can cater to a wide range of niches and interests, allowing for highly personalized and curated experiences.

Business Opportunities: Entrepreneurs can create subscription box businesses in various industries, tapping into a growing market.

Marketing and Brand Building: Subscription boxes can serve as a powerful marketing tool, helping brands gain exposure and build a loyal customer base.

How Starting a Subscription Box Service Works

Starting a subscription box service involves several key steps:

Niche Selection: Choose a specific niche or theme for your subscription box, such as gourmet coffee, pet toys, or self-care products.

Product Sourcing: Find suppliers or manufacturers for the products you'll include in your subscription box.

Box Design and Branding: Create eye-catching packaging and branding materials that resonate with your target audience.

Pricing and Subscription Plans: Determine pricing for your subscription plans and offer different subscription options (e.g., monthly, quarterly, annually).

Website and E-commerce Platform: Set up an e-commerce website where customers can subscribe to your service and manage their accounts.

Marketing and Promotion: Promote your subscription box through online marketing, social media, email marketing, and partnerships.

Order Fulfillment: Assemble and ship subscription boxes to subscribers on a regular schedule.

Responsibilities of Subscription Box Business Owners

Owners of subscription box businesses have various responsibilities:

Product Curation: Carefully select and curate products that align with your box's theme and provide value to subscribers.

Customer Support: Provide excellent customer support, addressing inquiries, feedback, and subscription management.

Logistics and Inventory: Manage inventory, shipping logistics, and supplier relationships.

Marketing and Growth: Continuously market your subscription box to attract and retain subscribers.

Financial Management: Handle billing, invoicing, and financial records.

Challenges in Starting a Subscription Box Service

Starting a subscription box service presents its own set of challenges:

Competition: The subscription box market is competitive, with many niche players and established brands.

Product Sourcing: Finding reliable suppliers and negotiating favorable terms can be challenging.

Customer Acquisition: Attracting and retaining subscribers in a competitive market requires effective marketing strategies.

Logistics and Fulfillment: Managing inventory and shipping logistics can be complex, especially as your subscriber base grows.

Compensation in Subscription Box Services

The compensation in a subscription box service business varies based on factors such as niche, pricing structure, and the number of subscribers. Subscription box businesses generate revenue primarily through monthly subscription fees.

Profits can range from a few hundred to several thousand dollars per month, depending on factors such as the number of subscribers, pricing strategy, and product cost.

Starting a subscription box service offers entrepreneurs a creative and potentially lucrative business opportunity. While it involves careful planning, product curation, and marketing efforts, the ability to create personalized experiences for subscribers and build a loyal customer base can be highly rewarding. Subscription box businesses continue to thrive as they cater to consumers' desire for convenience, novelty, and curated products delivered directly to their doorsteps.

TAX PREPARATION

Tax Preparation: Navigating Financial Compliance and Opportunities

Tax preparation is a vital financial service that individuals and businesses rely on to ensure compliance with tax laws and to maximize tax efficiency. Tax preparers assist clients in completing and filing their tax returns accurately and on time. In this page, we'll explore the world of tax preparation, its significance, how it works, responsibilities, challenges, and the potential compensation involved.

The Significance of Tax Preparation

Tax preparation holds significance for several reasons:

Legal Compliance: It ensures that individuals and businesses comply with tax laws, avoiding penalties and legal issues.

Financial Optimization: Tax preparers help clients identify tax deductions and credits, potentially reducing their tax liability and increasing their refunds.

Time and Stress Reduction: Outsourcing tax preparation saves clients time and reduces the stress associated with complex tax forms and regulations.

Business Efficiency: For businesses, accurate tax preparation is crucial for maintaining financial records and budgeting.

How Tax Preparation Works

Tax preparation involves several key steps:

Client Information Gathering: Tax preparers collect relevant financial information from clients, including income, expenses, deductions, and credits.

Documentation Review: They review tax-related documents such as W-2s, 1099s, and receipts.

Data Entry and Calculation: Tax preparers enter data into tax preparation software, calculate tax liability, and identify potential deductions and credits.

Filing: After reviewing the completed tax return with the client, they file it electronically or by mail, ensuring it meets deadlines and compliance requirements.

Communication: Tax preparers communicate with clients to answer questions, provide tax advice, and offer year-round support.

Responsibilities of Tax Preparers

Tax preparers have various responsibilities:

Client Consultation: Providing clients with personalized tax advice and strategies to minimize their tax liability.

Accuracy and Compliance: Ensuring that tax returns are accurate and comply with federal and state tax laws.

Record Keeping: Maintaining records of client tax information and returns for compliance and future reference.

Continuing Education: Staying updated on tax laws and regulations through ongoing training and education.

Challenges in Tax Preparation

Tax preparation comes with its own set of challenges:

Complexity: Tax laws are complex and subject to change, requiring tax preparers to stay informed and adaptable.

Client Expectations: Meeting client expectations for maximum refunds while maintaining compliance can be challenging.

Regulatory Risks: Mistakes in tax preparation can result in legal and financial consequences.

Compensation in Tax Preparation

The compensation in tax preparation varies based on factors such as location, level of expertise, the complexity of tax returns, and the number of clients served. Tax preparers may charge clients on an hourly basis, a flat fee per return, or a percentage of the refund.

Hourly rates for tax preparers typically range from $30 to $300 or more, depending on their experience and the complexity of the tax return. Some tax preparers also offer additional services, such as tax planning and financial consulting, which can command higher fees.

Tax preparation is an essential financial service that provides individuals and businesses with the expertise they need to navigate the complexities of tax laws and regulations. While it requires a deep understanding of tax codes, dedication to accuracy, and continuous learning, tax preparers play a crucial role in ensuring compliance and helping clients optimize their financial outcomes. The potential for compensation in tax preparation is influenced by expertise, client base, and the range of services offered, making it a rewarding field for those with the necessary skills and knowledge.

COURIER SERVICE

Courier or Delivery Services: Delivering Convenience and Efficiency

Courier and delivery services play a vital role in today's fast-paced world, facilitating the efficient movement of goods and documents from one location to another. Whether it's delivering packages, food, or important documents, courier services are essential for individuals and businesses. In this page, we'll explore the world of courier and delivery services, its significance, how it works, responsibilities, challenges, and the potential compensation involved.

The Significance of Courier and Delivery Services

Courier and delivery services hold significance for several reasons:

Convenience: They provide a convenient way for individuals and businesses to send and receive items without the need for in-person transportation.

Time-Sensitive: Courier services are often used for time-sensitive deliveries, such as legal documents or medical supplies.

E-commerce: The growth of e-commerce has increased the demand for courier services, especially in the parcel delivery sector.

Business Efficiency: Many businesses rely on courier services to streamline their supply chains and ensure timely delivery of products and materials.

How Courier and Delivery Services Work

Courier and delivery services involve several key steps:

Package Pickup: Couriers or delivery drivers collect packages or items from the sender's location.

Transportation: They transport the items to the destination, often using various modes of transportation, including bicycles, cars, vans, or even drones.

Tracking: Many courier services offer tracking capabilities so senders and recipients can monitor the progress of their deliveries in real-time.

Delivery: Couriers or drivers deliver the items to the recipient's location, obtaining signatures or confirmation as necessary.

Returns: Some courier services also handle returns, ensuring that items are sent back to the sender.

Responsibilities of Courier and Delivery Workers

Couriers and delivery workers have various responsibilities:

Timeliness: Ensuring that deliveries are made promptly and according to schedule.

Security: Safeguarding the items being transported to prevent damage or loss.

Communication: Providing updates to both senders and recipients about the status of deliveries.

Documentation: Maintaining records and documentation of deliveries for tracking and legal purposes.

Challenges in Courier and Delivery Services

Courier and delivery services face various challenges:

Traffic and Delays: Navigating traffic and dealing with delays can impact delivery schedules.

Security: Protecting packages from theft or damage during transit is a constant concern.

Weather Conditions: Adverse weather conditions can disrupt deliveries.

Compensation in Courier and Delivery Services

The compensation in courier and delivery services varies based on factors such as the type of deliveries, location, and employment status (employee or independent contractor).

Couriers: Couriers who work for courier companies or as independent contractors often earn an hourly wage or a fee per delivery, which can range from $10 to $25 or more per hour, depending on location and demand.

Delivery Drivers: Delivery drivers, especially those working for companies like food delivery services, may earn a combination of an hourly wage, tips, and delivery incentives. Earnings can vary widely but often amount to $15 to $30 per hour or more.

Independent Couriers: Independent couriers or owner-operators of delivery vehicles may have higher earning potential, especially if they serve commercial clients with regular, high-volume deliveries.

Courier and delivery services are an integral part of modern life, providing convenience and efficiency for individuals and businesses alike. While the work can be fast-paced and challenging, it offers a range of compensation opportunities depending on the specific role, location, and type of deliveries. The demand for courier and delivery services is expected to continue growing, making it a viable career option for those who enjoy staying on the move and ensuring that packages and items reach their destinations safely and on time.

T-SHIRT PRINTING

T-Shirt Printing: Bringing Creativity to Life, One Shirt at a Time

T-shirt printing is a dynamic and creative industry that allows individuals and businesses to express themselves through custom-designed apparel. Whether it's for personal use, promotional purposes, or starting a clothing brand, t-shirt printing has become a popular and accessible business venture. In this page, we'll explore the world of t-shirt printing, its significance, how it works, responsibilities, challenges, and the potential compensation involved.

The Significance of T-Shirt Printing

T-shirt printing holds significance for several reasons:

Personal Expression: It allows individuals to wear clothing that reflects their unique style, interests, and beliefs.

Branding and Marketing: Businesses use custom t-shirt printing for promotional purposes, creating branded merchandise and enhancing their visibility.

Artistic Expression: T-shirt printing serves as a canvas for artists and designers to showcase their creativity and designs.

Community Building: Custom t-shirts are often used to build a sense of belonging within groups, teams, or organizations.

How T-Shirt Printing Works

T-shirt printing involves several key steps:

Design Creation: A design is created using graphic design software or customized based on the client's preferences.

Color Separation: If necessary, the design is separated into individual colors to prepare for the printing process.

Printing Method: Various printing methods are used, including screen printing, direct-to-garment (DTG) printing, heat transfer, vinyl cutting, and sublimation.

Printing: The design is applied to the t-shirt using the chosen printing method, which may involve special inks, heat, or pressure.

Curing: In some methods, the printed t-shirt is cured using heat to set the ink and ensure durability.

Quality Control: The finished t-shirt is inspected for print quality and accuracy.

Responsibilities of T-Shirt Printing Business Owners

Owners of t-shirt printing businesses have various responsibilities:

Client Interaction: Communicating with clients to understand their design preferences, needs, and deadlines.

Design Execution: Ensuring that the chosen printing method and design accurately represent the client's vision.

Production Management: Overseeing the printing process, including equipment maintenance and quality control.

Inventory Management: Managing inventory of blank t-shirts, inks, and other supplies.

Marketing and Promotion: Promoting the business through online and offline marketing efforts.

Challenges in T-Shirt Printing

T-shirt printing comes with its own set of challenges:

Competition: The industry is competitive, with numerous t-shirt printing businesses offering similar services.

Design and Innovation: Staying creative and innovative to stand out in a crowded market.

Equipment and Technology: Keeping up with advances in printing technology and maintaining printing equipment.

Compensation in T-Shirt Printing

The compensation in t-shirt printing varies based on factors such as location, printing method, client base, and volume of orders.

Custom T-Shirt Printing: For custom t-shirt printing services, businesses typically charge clients based on the complexity of the design, the number of colors, and the quantity of shirts ordered. Prices per shirt can range from $10 to $30 or more.

Merchandise Sales: Some t-shirt printing businesses also create their own branded merchandise or clothing lines, generating revenue from sales to customers.

T-shirt printing is a vibrant and creative industry that enables individuals and businesses to express themselves, promote their brands, and showcase their artistic talents. While it requires skill, creativity, and business acumen, the potential for compensation in t-shirt printing is influenced by factors such as the printing method used, the volume of orders, and the pricing strategy. As custom apparel continues to be a popular choice for individuals and organizations, t-shirt printing businesses have the opportunity to thrive and bring creative visions to life, one shirt at a time.

DJING

DJing: Spinning Beats and Creating Musical Vibes

DJing is a dynamic and exhilarating profession that revolves around music, entertainment, and the art of mixing and blending tracks to create memorable experiences for audiences. Whether it's at a nightclub, music festival, wedding, or private event, DJs play a pivotal role in setting the mood and keeping the party alive. In this page, we'll explore the world of DJing, its significance, how it works, responsibilities, challenges, and the potential compensation involved.

The Significance of DJing

DJing holds significance for several reasons:

Musical Ambiance: DJs curate playlists and mixes that elevate the ambiance of any event, from dance parties to weddings.

Entertainment: They entertain and engage audiences by seamlessly transitioning between tracks and reading the crowd's energy.

Artistic Expression: DJing is a form of artistic expression, allowing DJs to showcase their unique musical tastes and styles.

Music Discovery: DJs introduce audiences to new music and genres, helping emerging artists gain recognition.

How DJing Works

DJing involves several key steps:

Music Selection: DJs carefully choose tracks that match the event's theme, mood, and audience preferences.

Mixing and Blending: They use turntables, mixers, and DJ software to mix and blend tracks together, creating a seamless and continuous music experience.

Beat matching: DJs synchronize the beats of two tracks to ensure a smooth transition.

Effects and Creativity: They incorporate effects, loops, and samples to add creative flair to their mixes.

Reading the Crowd: DJs assess the audience's response and adjust their playlists and mixes accordingly to keep the energy high.

Equipment Mastery: Mastering DJ equipment, such as turntables, mixers, controllers, and software, is crucial.

Responsibilities of DJs

DJs have various responsibilities:

Client Consultation: Understanding the client's musical preferences and event requirements.

Playlist Curation: Creating playlists or sets that match the event's theme or mood.

Performance: Delivering a captivating performance that keeps the audience engaged and entertained.

Equipment Maintenance: Ensuring that DJ equipment is well-maintained and functioning properly.

Promotion: Marketing and promoting their DJ services to secure bookings.

Challenges in DJing

DJing comes with its own set of challenges:

Competition: The industry can be highly competitive, with many DJs vying for gigs.

Music Knowledge: Staying up-to-date with music trends and discovering new tracks requires continuous effort.

Performance Pressure: Performing live in front of an audience can be stressful, requiring confidence and crowd-reading skills.

Compensation in DJing

The compensation in DJing varies widely based on several factors:

Experience: Experienced DJs often command higher fees than newcomers.

Event Type: The type of event (e.g., weddings, nightclubs, festivals) can influence the fee.

Location: DJs in larger cities or popular nightlife destinations may have more opportunities and higher earning potential.

Duration: Fees can also depend on the length of the performance.

Fees: DJ fees can range from $100 to several thousand dollars or more per event, depending on the factors mentioned above.

DJing is a thrilling and rewarding profession that allows individuals to share their passion for music and create unforgettable experiences for audiences. While it requires musical knowledge, technical skills, and the ability to adapt to different crowds and events, the potential for compensation is influenced by factors such as experience, location, and the type of events DJs are booked for. As the demand for live music experiences and entertainment remains strong, DJing continues to be a vibrant and sought-after career for music enthusiasts.

SOCIAL MEDIA MARKETING COMPANY

Starting a Social Media Marketing Company: Navigating the Digital Marketing Landscape

Starting a social media marketing company is a dynamic and promising entrepreneurial venture that allows you to leverage the power of social media platforms to help businesses grow their online presence and reach a wider audience. In today's digital age, businesses recognize the importance of a strong social media presence, making social media marketing a thriving industry. In this page, we'll explore the world of starting a social media marketing company, its significance, how it works, responsibilities, challenges, and the potential compensation involved.

The Significance of Social Media Marketing

Social media marketing holds significance for several reasons:

Online Presence: It helps businesses establish and maintain an active online presence, which is crucial for brand visibility and customer engagement.

Audience Reach: Social media platforms provide access to vast and diverse audiences, allowing businesses to target specific demographics.

Customer Engagement: Social media fosters direct communication with customers, enabling businesses to build relationships and gather feedback.

Data and Analytics: Social media marketing offers valuable data and analytics tools for measuring performance and refining strategies.

How Starting a Social Media Marketing Company Works

Starting a social media marketing company involves several key steps:

Business Planning: Develop a comprehensive business plan outlining your niche, target market, services offered, pricing structure, and marketing strategies.

Legal Considerations: Register your business, obtain necessary licenses, and ensure compliance with data protection and privacy laws.

Skills and Expertise: Acquire the necessary skills and expertise in social media marketing, including knowledge of various platforms, advertising, content creation, and analytics.

Team Building: As your business grows, consider building a team of social media experts, content creators, and analysts.

Client Acquisition: Attract clients through marketing efforts, referrals, and a portfolio showcasing your previous successful campaigns.

Service Delivery: Offer a range of social media marketing services, including content creation, advertising, audience engagement, and analytics.

Responsibilities of Social Media Marketing Company Owners

Owners of social media marketing companies have various responsibilities:

Client Consultation: Understand clients' goals, target audience, and branding to develop effective social media strategies.

Campaign Management: Plan and execute social media campaigns, including content creation, posting schedules, and advertising.

Data Analysis: Use analytics tools to monitor campaign performance, make data-driven decisions, and report results to clients.

Team Management: If you have a team, manage their tasks, schedules, and performance to ensure successful campaign execution.

Financial Management: Handle billing, invoicing, and financial records.

Challenges in Starting a Social Media Marketing Company

Starting a social media marketing company presents its own set of challenges:

Competition: The industry is highly competitive, with many agencies offering similar services.

Algorithm Changes: Frequent changes in social media algorithms can impact campaign performance.

Client Expectations: Meeting client expectations and delivering measurable results can be challenging.

Compensation in Social Media Marketing

The compensation in a social media marketing company varies based on several factors, including location, the scale of the campaigns, services offered, and the size of the client portfolio.

Pricing Structure: Social media marketing companies typically charge clients on a monthly retainer or project-based fee. Monthly retainer fees can range from a few hundred to several thousand dollars, while project-based fees depend on the scope and complexity of the campaign.

Profit Margin: Profit margins can vary widely based on overhead costs, client acquisition, and the efficiency of campaign management. Successful companies can achieve healthy profit margins.

Starting a social media marketing company is a rewarding way to help businesses thrive in the digital age. While it requires expertise, strategic thinking, and the ability to adapt to evolving social media trends, the potential for compensation is significant, especially as businesses increasingly recognize the importance of a strong online presence. Social media marketing companies play a crucial role in helping businesses connect with their target audiences and achieve their digital marketing goals, making it a valuable and dynamic industry to be part of.

E-COMMERCE STORE

E-commerce Store: Building Digital Marketplaces and Online Success

Starting an e-commerce store is a dynamic and versatile entrepreneurial venture that enables individuals and businesses to sell products and services online. E-commerce has revolutionized the way we shop, making it convenient for consumers to browse, purchase, and receive goods without leaving their homes. In this page, we'll explore the world of starting an e-commerce store, its significance, how it works, responsibilities, challenges, and the potential compensation involved.

The Significance of E-commerce Stores

E-commerce stores hold significance for several reasons:

Convenience: They offer consumers the convenience of shopping anytime, anywhere, without the constraints of physical store hours.

Global Reach: E-commerce stores can reach a global audience, breaking down geographical barriers.

Business Opportunities: Entrepreneurs can start e-commerce businesses in various niches and industries, capitalizing on online consumer demand.

Cost Efficiency: Operating an e-commerce store can be more cost-effective than maintaining a physical storefront.

How E-commerce Stores Work

Starting an e-commerce store involves several key steps:

Niche Selection: Choose a specific niche or industry for your online store, considering market demand and competition.

Product Sourcing: Find reliable suppliers or manufacturers for the products you plan to sell.

Website Creation: Create an e-commerce website or online store using platforms like Shopify, WooCommerce, or Magento.

Product Listings: Upload product listings, including images, descriptions, prices, and availability.

Payment and Checkout: Set up secure payment processing and checkout options for customers.

Website Optimization: Optimize your website for search engines (SEO) and user experience (UX) to attract and retain customers.

Marketing and Promotion: Promote your e-commerce store through digital marketing channels, including social media, email marketing, and paid advertising.

Order Fulfillment: Efficiently process and ship orders to customers, ensuring timely delivery.

Responsibilities of E-commerce Store Owners

Owners of e-commerce stores have various responsibilities:

Product Selection: Curating and selecting products to offer in the online store.

Website Maintenance: Regularly updating and maintaining the e-commerce website, including product listings and security features.

Customer Service: Providing customer support, addressing inquiries, and managing returns and refunds.

Inventory Management: Managing inventory levels and restocking products as needed.

Digital Marketing: Running marketing campaigns to attract and retain customers.

Challenges in E-commerce

Starting an e-commerce store presents its own set of challenges:

Competition: The e-commerce market is highly competitive, with many online stores vying for consumer attention.

Digital Marketing: Effectively marketing the online store and driving traffic can be challenging, especially for newcomers.

Logistics: Managing shipping, inventory, and order fulfillment can be complex, particularly as the business grows.

Compensation in E-commerce

The compensation in e-commerce varies widely based on factors such as the niche, product pricing, marketing efforts, and the scale of the e-commerce store.

Sales Revenue: E-commerce store owners generate revenue primarily through sales. Profits can range from a few hundred to millions of dollars per year, depending on the scale and success of the store.

E-commerce Fees: E-commerce platforms may charge fees for using their services, which can impact profit margins.

Marketing Costs: Digital marketing costs, including advertising and promotions, can also affect profitability.

Starting an e-commerce store is a rewarding way to tap into the vast online consumer market and create a successful online business. While it requires careful planning, product selection, digital marketing expertise, and strong customer service, the potential for compensation in e-commerce is substantial. E-commerce stores continue to thrive as consumers increasingly turn to online shopping for convenience and a wide range of products, making it an exciting and dynamic industry for entrepreneurs to explore.

CATERING BUSINESS

Catering: Crafting Culinary Experiences and Feeding Celebrations

Catering is a versatile and fulfilling industry that involves preparing and serving food and beverages at events, parties, weddings, and corporate gatherings. Caterers are entrusted with creating memorable dining experiences that leave a lasting impression on guests. In this page, we'll explore the world of catering, its significance, how it works, responsibilities, challenges, and the potential compensation involved.

The Significance of Catering

Catering holds significance for several reasons:

Event Enhancement: It enhances events by providing a diverse menu, impeccable service, and a memorable dining experience.

Convenience: Catering allows hosts to focus on their guests and the event's program without worrying about food preparation and service.

Specialization: Caterers can specialize in various cuisines, dietary preferences, and themes, catering to diverse client needs.

Business Opportunities: Entrepreneurs can start catering businesses, tapping into the demand for professional catering services.

How Catering Works

Catering involves several key steps:

Client Consultation: Understanding the client's event, budget, dietary preferences, and menu expectations.

Menu Planning: Creating a customized menu that aligns with the event's theme and guest preferences.

Food Preparation: Carefully sourcing ingredients, preparing dishes, and ensuring food safety and hygiene.

Service Staff: Hiring and training service staff, including chefs, servers, and bartenders, as needed.

Event Setup: Arranging tables, chairs, linens, tableware, and decor to create an inviting dining environment.

Food Presentation: Ensuring dishes are beautifully presented to enhance the overall dining experience.

Service: Providing attentive and courteous service, including food and beverage service, to guests during the event.

Cleanup: Disassembling and cleaning up after the event, including proper food storage and disposal.

Responsibilities of Catering Business Owners

Owners of catering businesses have various responsibilities:

Client Relations: Building and maintaining client relationships, including consultations, menu planning, and event coordination.

Food Quality: Ensuring that food is prepared to the highest quality and safety standards.

Team Management: Managing catering teams, including hiring, training, and scheduling.

Logistics and Inventory: Managing inventory, equipment, and logistics for multiple events.

Marketing and Promotion: Promoting the catering business through marketing efforts, including a professional website, social media, and word-of-mouth referrals.

Challenges in Catering

Catering comes with its own set of challenges:

Event Variability: Each event is unique, and caterers must adapt to different client expectations, guest counts, and venues.

Logistics: Coordinating multiple events on the same day can be logistically challenging.

Food Safety: Maintaining strict food safety and hygiene standards is essential to prevent food borne illnesses.

Compensation in Catering

The compensation in catering varies based on factors such as location, the type of events catered, menu complexity, and the size of the catering business.

Pricing Structure: Caterers typically charge clients per person, with prices ranging from $20 to $150 or more per guest, depending on factors like the menu, service style, and event complexity.

Profit Margin: Profit margins in catering can vary based on overhead costs, ingredient quality, and pricing strategies. Successful catering businesses can achieve healthy profit margins.

Catering is a rewarding profession that allows culinary enthusiasts and entrepreneurs to craft culinary experiences and bring joy to celebrations. While it requires culinary expertise, strong management skills, and adaptability, the potential for compensation is influenced by factors such as location, event complexity, and pricing strategies. Caterers play a pivotal role in ensuring that events are not only well-organized but also memorable, leaving guests with a taste of culinary excellence and hospitality.

PODCASTING

Podcasting: Sharing Stories, Ideas, and Voices with the World

Starting a podcasting venture is an exciting and creative endeavor that allows individuals and organizations to share their thoughts, stories, and expertise with a global audience. Podcasting has gained immense popularity in recent years, offering a platform for diverse voices and topics. In this page, we'll explore the world of podcasting, its significance, how it works, responsibilities, challenges, and the potential compensation involved.

The Significance of Podcasting

Podcasting holds significance for several reasons:

Accessibility: It provides a platform for individuals and organizations to reach a global audience, irrespective of location or resources.

Diverse Content: Podcasts cover an array of topics, from news and education to entertainment and storytelling, catering to diverse interests.

Connection: Podcasts foster connections and communities, allowing listeners to engage with content creators and like-minded individuals.

Monetization: Podcasters have various monetization options, including advertising, sponsorships, merchandise sales, and listener support.

How Podcasting Works

Starting a podcast involves several key steps:

Topic Selection: Choose a niche or topic that aligns with your expertise or interests and appeals to a target audience.

Content Creation: Plan and create podcast episodes, including scripting, recording, and editing.

Equipment Setup: Acquire the necessary podcasting equipment, such as microphones, headphones, and recording software.

Hosting and Distribution: Choose a podcast hosting platform to store and distribute your episodes to podcast directories like Apple Podcasts, Spotify, and Google Podcasts.

Promotion: Market and promote your podcast through social media, email newsletters, and collaborations to expand your listener base.

Engagement: Engage with your audience through listener feedback, reviews, and community building.

Responsibilities of Podcasters

Podcasters have various responsibilities:

Content Planning: Creating engaging and informative content that resonates with the target audience.

Recording and Editing: Recording episodes, editing audio, and ensuring high audio quality.

Distribution: Uploading episodes to hosting platforms and directories.

Marketing and Promotion: Promoting the podcast to attract new listeners and sponsors.

Audience Engagement: Building and maintaining a connection with the listener community.

Challenges in Podcasting

Podcasting comes with its own set of challenges:

Content Consistency: Maintaining a regular episode schedule and consistently producing quality content can be demanding.

Visibility: Gaining visibility and growing a listener base in a competitive podcasting landscape can be challenging.

Monetization: Successfully monetizing a podcast may require time and strategic partnerships.

Compensation in Podcasting

The compensation in podcasting varies based on several factors, including audience size, monetization strategies, and industry niche.

Advertising and Sponsorships: Many podcasters earn revenue through advertising and sponsorships, with rates varying based on audience reach and niche. CPM (cost per thousand downloads) rates can range from $15 to $50 or more.

Listener Support: Some podcasters rely on listener support platforms like Patreon, where listeners contribute a monthly fee to access exclusive content and benefits.

Merchandise Sales: Podcasters often sell merchandise related to their podcasts, such as t-shirts, mugs, or books.

Live Shows and Events: Successful podcasts may host live shows or events, generating revenue from ticket sales and merchandise.

Podcasting offers a creative and accessible way to share stories, ideas, and expertise with a global audience. While it requires dedication, content creation skills, and marketing efforts to build an audience, the potential for compensation in podcasting is substantial, with multiple monetization avenues available. As the podcasting industry continues to evolve and expand, it remains an exciting and promising medium for content creators and storytellers to connect with audiences and share their voices with the world.

DROP SHIPPING

Drop shipping: Simplifying E-commerce with Minimal Risk

Starting a dropshipping business is a popular and accessible way to venture into e-commerce without the need for significant upfront investments in inventory. Dropshipping allows entrepreneurs to sell products online without physically stocking them. Instead, the products are shipped directly from suppliers to customers. In this page, we'll explore the world of dropshipping, its significance, how it works, responsibilities, challenges, and the potential compensation involved.

The Significance of Dropshipping

Dropshipping holds significance for several reasons:

Low Startup Costs: Entrepreneurs can start a dropshipping business with minimal upfront expenses, making it an accessible option for newcomers to e-commerce.

Inventory Management: Dropshipping eliminates the need for inventory storage, reducing overhead costs and risks associated with unsold stock.

Product Variety: Dropshippers can offer a wide range of products from different suppliers, catering to diverse customer preferences.

Location Independence: Dropshipping businesses can be operated from anywhere with an internet connection, offering flexibility and freedom.

How Dropshipping Works

Starting a dropshipping business involves several key steps:

Niche Selection: Choose a niche or industry for your online store, considering market demand and competition.

Supplier Selection: Find reliable suppliers or manufacturers willing to dropship their products. Popular platforms like AliExpress, SaleHoo, and Oberlo are commonly used.

Online Store Setup: Create an e-commerce website or online store using platforms like Shopify, WooCommerce, or Magento.

Product Listings: Import or create product listings on your website, including images, descriptions, prices, and availability.

Order Management: When customers place orders on your website, forward the order details to the supplier for fulfillment.

Customer Service: Provide customer support, address inquiries, and manage returns and refunds.

Marketing and Promotion: Promote your dropshipping store through digital marketing channels to attract customers.

Responsibilities of Dropshipping Business Owners

Owners of dropshipping businesses have various responsibilities:

Supplier Relations: Building and maintaining relationships with suppliers, including negotiation of terms and pricing.

Website Management: Regularly updating and maintaining the e-commerce website, including product listings and security features.

Customer Relations: Providing excellent customer service to ensure customer satisfaction and repeat business.

Marketing: Running marketing campaigns to attract and retain customers, including social media marketing, email marketing, and paid advertising.

Challenges in Dropshipping

Starting a dropshipping business presents its own set of challenges:

Supplier Reliability: Dependence on suppliers for product quality and timely order fulfillment can be a risk.

Competition: The e-commerce market is highly competitive, with many dropshipping stores vying for consumer attention.

Marketing Efforts: Effectively marketing the dropshipping store and driving traffic can be challenging, especially for newcomers.

Compensation in Dropshipping

The compensation in dropshipping varies widely based on several factors, including niche selection, marketing efforts, and the scale of the dropshipping business.

Profit Margin: Profit margins in dropshipping can be modest, typically ranging from 10% to 30% or more, depending on the products and suppliers used.

Volume of Sales: Higher sales volumes can translate to greater revenue and profit potential.

Marketing Costs: Expenses related to digital marketing and advertising can impact profitability.

Dropshipping offers an accessible and low-risk entry into the world of e-commerce, allowing entrepreneurs to start online businesses with minimal upfront investments. While it requires careful supplier selection, effective marketing, and customer service efforts to succeed, the potential for compensation in dropshipping is influenced by factors such as niche selection and business scale. As e-commerce continues to thrive and evolve, dropshipping remains a promising avenue for entrepreneurs looking to explore online retail without the burdens of traditional inventory management.

VIRTUAL ASSISTANT

Virtual Assistant: The Remote Support Superstars

Becoming a virtual assistant (VA) is a versatile and rewarding career choice that allows individuals to provide a wide range of administrative, creative, and technical support services to clients from around the world. Virtual assistants play a crucial role in helping businesses and entrepreneurs manage their tasks and projects remotely, enabling them to focus on their core activities. In this page, we'll explore the world of virtual assistance, its significance, how it works, responsibilities, challenges, and the potential compensation involved.

The Significance of Virtual Assistance

Virtual assistants hold significance for several reasons:

Remote Support: They offer remote support, making it possible for businesses to access skilled professionals from anywhere.

Time and Cost Savings: VAs help clients save time and reduce operational costs by outsourcing tasks and projects.

Expertise: Virtual assistants often have specialized skills, from administrative tasks to graphic design, which can benefit businesses of all sizes.

Work-Life Balance: For VAs, it provides an opportunity to work flexibly and balance their personal and professional lives.

How Virtual Assistance Works

Becoming a virtual assistant involves several key steps:

Skill Development: Acquire skills relevant to the services you intend to offer, such as administrative support, social media management, content writing, or graphic design.

Market Research: Identify your target market and potential clients who require your services.

Online Presence: Create a professional online presence through a website, social media profiles, and a portfolio showcasing your skills and previous work.

Client Acquisition: Attract clients through marketing efforts, networking, and referrals.

Service Delivery: Provide high-quality services to clients remotely, communicating through email, messaging apps, and project management tools.

Responsibilities of Virtual Assistants

Virtual assistants have various responsibilities:

Client Communication: Maintain clear and effective communication with clients to understand their needs and requirements.

Task Management: Manage tasks and projects assigned by clients efficiently and within specified timelines.

Organization: Keep track of schedules, appointments, and deadlines, ensuring that all tasks are completed on time.

Technical Skills: Utilize various software and tools to perform tasks, such as project management software, Microsoft Office, or graphic design software.

Confidentiality: Maintain client confidentiality and data security.

Challenges in Virtual Assistance

Virtual assistance comes with its own set of challenges:

Client Acquisition: Acquiring clients and building a client base can be challenging, especially for new VAs.

Remote Work: Staying organized and productive while working remotely requires discipline and time management skills.

Variability: The types of tasks and projects assigned by clients can vary widely, requiring adaptability and versatility.

Compensation in Virtual Assistance

The compensation in virtual assistance varies based on several factors, including experience, specialization, and the types of services offered.

Pricing Structure: Virtual assistants typically charge clients on an hourly, project-based, or retainer basis. Hourly rates can range from $15 to $50 or more, depending on the VA's skills and expertise.

Experience: Experienced VAs often command higher rates than newcomers.

Specialization: Specialized skills, such as digital marketing, graphic design, or web development, can lead to higher fees.

Becoming a virtual assistant is a versatile and valuable career choice that offers the flexibility to work remotely while providing essential support to businesses and entrepreneurs. While it requires skill development, effective client acquisition, and time management, the potential for compensation in virtual assistance is influenced by factors such as experience, specialization, and pricing structure. As businesses continue to seek remote support and expertise, virtual assistants play a pivotal role in helping them thrive and succeed in today's digital age.

ONLINE TUTORING

Online Tutoring: Empowering Minds and Shaping Futures

Online tutoring is a dynamic and impactful profession that allows educators and subject matter experts to share their knowledge and expertise with students worldwide through digital platforms. This form of remote education has gained significant popularity, providing personalized learning experiences and academic support. In this page, we'll explore the world of online tutoring, its significance, how it works, responsibilities, challenges, and the potential compensation involved.

The Significance of Online Tutoring

Online tutoring holds significance for several reasons:

Accessibility: It offers students access to a wide range of subjects and expertise, regardless of their geographical location.

Personalization: Online tutoring can be highly personalized to meet the specific needs and learning styles of individual students.

Convenience: Both students and tutors benefit from the convenience of scheduling lessons and studying from the comfort of their own homes.

Global Reach: Online tutoring allows tutors to reach a global audience and students to connect with educators from around the world.

How Online Tutoring Works

Participating in online tutoring involves several key steps:

Expertise: Develop expertise in the subject or field you plan to tutor, whether it's academic subjects, test preparation, language learning, or specialized skills.

Online Platform: Choose an online tutoring platform or set up your own website for offering tutoring services.

Profile Creation: Create a professional online profile that showcases your qualifications, experience, teaching style, and availability.

Student Acquisition: Attract students through marketing efforts, word-of-mouth referrals, or by joining tutoring platforms.

Scheduling: Coordinate lesson schedules with students, taking into account time zones and availability.

Teaching: Conduct online tutoring sessions through video conferencing, virtual whiteboards, and other digital tools.

Assessment and Feedback: Provide constructive feedback to students, track their progress, and adapt lesson plans accordingly.

Responsibilities of Online Tutors

Online tutors have various responsibilities:

Subject Mastery: Maintain a deep understanding of the subject matter and stay updated with relevant curriculum changes.

Pedagogical Skills: Develop effective teaching strategies and adapt to students' learning needs.

Communication: Establish clear and effective communication with students, addressing their questions and concerns.

Scheduling: Manage lesson schedules, ensuring punctuality and reliability.

Assessment: Assess students' progress through assignments, quizzes, and tests.

Challenges in Online Tutoring

Online tutoring comes with its own set of challenges:

Technology: Both tutors and students need access to reliable technology and a stable internet connection.

Adaptability: Adapting teaching methods to the online environment and different learning styles can be a learning curve.

Competition: The online tutoring market can be competitive, especially for popular subjects.

Compensation in Online Tutoring

The compensation in online tutoring varies based on several factors, including the subject, expertise, and the platform used.

Pricing Structure: Online tutors may charge students on an hourly basis or offer packages of lessons. Hourly rates can range from $20 to $100 or more, depending on the subject and tutor's experience.

Specialization: Tutors with expertise in high-demand fields, such as test preparation or specialized skills (e.g., coding, music), can command higher fees.

Online tutoring is a powerful and flexible profession that allows educators and experts to make a meaningful impact on students' lives while leveraging the convenience and accessibility of digital platforms. While it requires subject mastery, effective teaching skills, and adaptability to the online environment, the potential for compensation in online tutoring is influenced by factors such as specialization, subject demand, and pricing structure. As education continues to evolve in the digital age, online tutors play a pivotal role in empowering students to achieve their academic goals and unlock their full potential.

RENTING YOUR CAR

Renting Out Your Car: Earning from Your Idle Asset

Renting out your personal vehicle through car-sharing apps has become an increasingly popular way for car owners to earn extra income. This sharing economy model allows individuals to make their cars available for rent when they're not using them, providing a cost-effective and convenient transportation option for renters. In this page, we'll explore the world of renting out your car using apps, its significance, how it works, responsibilities, challenges, and the potential compensation involved.

The Significance of Car-Sharing Apps

Car-sharing apps hold significance for several reasons:

Asset Monetization: Car owners can earn income by renting out their vehicles during periods of inactivity, offsetting ownership costs.

Affordable Transportation: Renters benefit from access to a variety of vehicles without the commitment and expense of ownership.

Environmental Impact: Car-sharing reduces the need for private car ownership, potentially reducing traffic congestion and carbon emissions.

Urban Mobility: Car-sharing is especially valuable in urban areas where public transportation may be limited or inconvenient.

How Car-Sharing Apps Work

Participating in car-sharing involves several key steps:

Platform Registration: Car owners register on car-sharing platforms such as Turo, Getaround, or Zipcar, providing details about their vehicle.

Vehicle Listing: Owners create listings for their cars, including photos, descriptions, availability, and pricing.

Renter Booking: Renters browse available vehicles on the platform, select one that meets their needs, and book it for a specified duration.

Key Handover: Owners and renters coordinate the vehicle handover, which may involve in-person key exchange or keyless entry through the app.

Usage: Renters use the car for their intended purpose, adhering to the terms and conditions set by the platform.

Return and Payment: Renters return the car at the agreed-upon time and location. Payment is handled through the platform, with owners receiving a share of the rental fee.

Responsibilities of Car Owners

Car owners participating in car-sharing have various responsibilities:

Vehicle Maintenance: Ensuring the car is well-maintained and safe for renters to use.

Cleanliness: Providing a clean and tidy vehicle for renters.

Availability: Making the car available during the scheduled rental periods.

Communication: Maintaining clear communication with renters, including coordinating pick-up and drop-off.

Challenges in Car-Sharing

Car-sharing comes with its own set of challenges:

Vehicle Wear and Tear: Renting out your car can lead to increased wear and tear, which may require more frequent maintenance.

Insurance: Car-sharing platforms typically provide insurance coverage, but owners should understand the terms and conditions to ensure they have adequate protection.

Legal and Regulatory Considerations: Compliance with local regulations and taxation may be required.

Compensation in Car-Sharing

The compensation in car-sharing varies based on several factors:

Pricing Structure: Owners set their own rental rates based on factors such as the vehicle type, location, and demand. Daily rates can range from $20 to $200 or more, with owners typically earning a percentage (60-80%) of the rental fee.

Vehicle Demand: Owners with high-demand vehicles in popular locations may have more frequent bookings and higher earnings.

Availability: The more available a vehicle is for rental, the higher the potential for earnings.

Renting out your car through car-sharing apps offers an opportunity to earn extra income from an idle asset while providing renters with affordable and convenient transportation options. While it requires responsible vehicle ownership, maintenance, and adherence to platform policies, the potential for compensation in car-sharing is influenced by factors such as vehicle type, location, and pricing. As the sharing economy continues to grow, car-sharing represents a flexible and accessible way for car owners to put their vehicles to work and contribute to more sustainable urban mobility.

PRINT ON DEMAND

Print on Demand: Turning Creativity into Profit

Print on demand (POD) is a revolutionary business model that empowers artists, designers, entrepreneurs, and content creators to transform their ideas into physical products without the need for upfront investments in inventory. This on-demand printing process allows for the creation of custom-designed merchandise, from clothing to home decor, in response to customer orders. In this page, we'll explore the world of print on demand, its significance, how it works, responsibilities, challenges, and the potential compensation involved.

The Significance of Print on Demand

Print on demand holds significance for several reasons:

Creativity: It allows individuals to express their creativity by designing and selling custom merchandise.

Cost Efficiency: POD eliminates the need for inventory storage, reducing overhead costs and the risk of unsold products.

Entrepreneurship: Entrepreneurs can start POD businesses with minimal upfront investments and expand their product offerings over time.

Customization: Customers can purchase personalized products, adding a unique touch to their purchases.

How Print on Demand Works

Participating in print on demand involves several key steps:

Design Creation: Artists and designers create custom designs, artwork, or graphics for various product types, such as t-shirts, posters, or mugs.

Product Selection: Sellers choose the products they want to offer and upload their designs to a POD platform or their online store.

Online Store Setup: Sellers may set up their own e-commerce websites or use POD platforms like Printful, Printify, or Teespring to create product listings.

Customer Orders: When customers place orders, the POD platform or seller's website sends the order details to a printing partner for production.

Printing and Fulfillment: The printing partner produces the custom products, handles quality control, and ships the items directly to the customers.

Customer Service: Sellers are responsible for providing customer support, addressing inquiries, and managing returns and refunds.

Responsibilities in Print on Demand

Individuals and businesses involved in print on demand have various responsibilities:

Design Creation: Creating unique and appealing designs that resonate with the target audience.

Quality Control: Ensuring the quality and accuracy of printed products before shipping to customers.

Marketing and Promotion: Promoting the products through digital marketing channels, social media, email marketing, and collaborations.

Customer Service: Providing excellent customer service, addressing inquiries, and managing returns and refunds.

Challenges in Print on Demand

Print on demand comes with its own set of challenges:

Design Competition: The market can be highly competitive, with many sellers offering similar products.

Quality Control: Ensuring consistent quality across printed products is crucial to maintaining customer satisfaction.

Marketing and Visibility: Effectively marketing the products and driving traffic to the online store can be challenging.

Compensation in Print on Demand

The compensation in print on demand varies based on several factors:

Pricing Structure: Sellers set their own pricing, taking into account production costs, platform fees, and desired profit margins. Profit margins per product can range from a few dollars to over $20, depending on the product type and pricing strategy.

Sales Volume: High sales volume can lead to greater earnings, especially for popular designs and products.

Marketing Efforts: Successful marketing and promotion efforts can drive more sales and increase revenue.

Print on demand offers a creative and accessible way for artists, designers, and entrepreneurs to turn their ideas into tangible products and generate income. While it requires strong design skills, marketing efforts, and a commitment to quality, the potential for compensation in print on demand is influenced by factors such as product selection, pricing strategy, and sales volume. As consumers seek personalized and unique products, print on demand continues to thrive as a dynamic and profitable business model in the world of e-commerce and creative entrepreneurship.

STARTING A DIGITAL MARKETING COMPANY

Starting Your Own Digital Marketing Company: A Guide to Success

In today's digital-centric world, businesses are increasingly seeking the expertise of digital marketing companies to help them navigate the complex online landscape, expand their reach, and drive growth. If you have a passion for marketing and an entrepreneurial spirit, starting your own digital marketing company can be a rewarding venture. In this guide, we'll explore the essential steps to launch your digital marketing agency, the challenges you might face, and the potential pay range you can expect.

Steps to Start a Digital Marketing Company

Market Research and Niche Selection: Begin by conducting thorough market research to identify your target audience, competitors, and potential niches. Specializing in a specific industry or marketing service can set you apart from the competition.

Business Plan: Create a detailed business plan outlining your agency's goals, services, pricing strategy, marketing plan, and financial projections. A well-crafted plan is crucial for securing funding and staying on track.

Legal Structure and Registration: Choose a legal structure for your business (e.g., sole proprietorship, LLC, corporation) and complete the necessary registrations and permits.

Branding and Online Presence: Develop a strong brand identity, including a memorable company name, logo, and website. Your online presence should showcase your expertise and attract potential clients.

Services Offered: Determine the range of digital marketing services your agency will offer, such as SEO, content marketing, social media management, PPC advertising, email marketing, and more.

Team Building: Hire skilled professionals with expertise in various digital marketing disciplines. Building a talented team is crucial for delivering high-quality services.

Client Acquisition: Develop a client acquisition strategy, which may include networking, cold outreach, content marketing, and partnerships. Building a strong client portfolio is essential for growth.

Client Servicing and Retention: Provide exceptional service to your clients to build trust and secure long-term relationships. Happy clients are more likely to refer your agency to others.

Tools and Technology: Invest in the necessary tools and software for effective digital marketing campaign management and analytics.

Compliance and Ethics: Stay informed about digital marketing regulations and ethical practices to ensure your agency operates ethically and legally.

Challenges and Considerations

While starting a digital marketing company can be rewarding, it also comes with its fair share of challenges:

Competition: The digital marketing industry is highly competitive, with numerous agencies vying for clients. Finding a unique selling proposition (USP) is vital.

Constant Learning: The digital marketing landscape evolves rapidly. To stay competitive, you and your team must continuously learn and adapt to new trends and technologies.

Client Expectations: Meeting and exceeding client expectations can be demanding. Effective communication and managing client expectations are essential.

Financial Stability: Building a client base and maintaining steady revenue can take time. Ensure you have sufficient financial reserves to cover initial expenses.

Regulatory Compliance: Stay up-to-date with digital marketing regulations, including data protection laws (e.g., GDPR, CCPA).

Pay Range in the Digital Marketing Industry

The pay range for digital marketing agencies can vary widely based on factors such as location, agency size, client portfolio, and services offered. As of my last knowledge update in September 2021, here's a rough estimate of the potential pay range for digital marketing agency owners:

Startup Phase (First Year): In the initial stages, agency owners might earn between $30,000 to $60,000 per year or even less, depending on the number of clients and services offered.

Growth Phase (2-5 Years): With successful client acquisition and expansion, agency owners can earn between $60,000 to $150,000 or more annually.

Established Agency (5+ Years): As your agency becomes well-established and acquires a substantial client base, the earning potential can range from $100,000 to several million dollars per year.

It's important to note that these figures are approximate and can vary widely. Success in the digital marketing industry depends on your ability to provide value to clients, build a strong brand, and adapt to industry changes.

Starting a digital marketing company is an exciting entrepreneurial endeavor that offers the potential for financial success and personal fulfillment. However, it's essential to approach it with careful planning, dedication, and a commitment to staying current in the ever-evolving digital landscape. While the initial phases may be financially challenging, with perseverance and a focus on delivering exceptional results, your agency can thrive and become a leading player in the digital marketing industry.

LIFE COACHING

Pursuing a Career in Life Coaching: Pathways and Pay Range

Life coaching is a dynamic and fulfilling profession that empowers individuals to achieve personal and professional growth. If you have a passion for helping others unlock their full potential, consider a career in life coaching. In this guide, we'll explore the steps to become a life coach, the various niches within the field, potential challenges, and the pay range you can expect as a life coach.

Steps to Becoming a Life Coach

Self-Reflection: Start by examining your own values, beliefs, and life experiences. A strong foundation in self-awareness will enable you to guide others effectively.

Training and Certification: While life coaching is an unregulated industry, many aspiring coaches pursue training programs and certification through accredited organizations like the International Coach Federation (ICF). These programs provide valuable skills, tools, and credibility.

Choose Your Niche: Life coaching encompasses a wide range of niches, including career coaching, relationship coaching, wellness coaching, and more. Identify your niche based on your interests and expertise.

Build Your Brand: Establish an online presence with a professional website and active social media profiles. Share valuable content and testimonials to showcase your expertise.

Client Acquisition: Develop strategies for attracting clients, which may include networking, offering free workshops or webinars, and collaborating with other professionals.

Initial Consultations: Conduct initial consultations to understand your clients' needs and goals. This step is essential for building a coaching plan tailored to each client.

Coaching Sessions: Conduct regular coaching sessions with your clients to help them set and achieve their goals. Effective communication and active listening are crucial skills.

Continuous Learning: Stay up-to-date with the latest coaching techniques and tools. Continued education and personal development are essential in this field.

Challenges and Considerations

As with any profession, life coaching comes with its challenges:

Building a Client Base: Attracting and retaining clients can be challenging, especially when you're just starting. Building a strong online presence and word-of-mouth referrals are key.

Client Progress: Not all clients will achieve their goals, and some may not fully engage in the coaching process. Managing client expectations and maintaining motivation can be demanding.

Income Variability: Income as a life coach can be variable, particularly in the early stages of your career. It may take time to establish a steady stream of clients.

Emotional Toll: Coaching often involves dealing with clients' personal challenges and emotional issues. Coaches need to establish boundaries and self-care routines.

Continuous Self-Improvement: The field of coaching evolves, and successful coaches must continually improve their skills and adapt to changes in client needs and expectations.

Pay Range in Life Coaching

The pay range for life coaches varies widely and depends on several factors, including location, niche, experience, and reputation. As of my last knowledge update in September 2021, here's a general overview of the potential pay range for life coaches:

Entry-Level Coaches: In the early stages of your coaching career, you may earn between $20,000 to $60,000 per year. Income can be lower while you build your client base and reputation.

Experienced Coaches: With several years of experience and a solid client base, experienced life coaches can earn between $60,000 to $150,000 or more annually.

Specialized Coaches: Coaches who specialize in high-demand niches, such as executive coaching or corporate coaching, can command higher fees, potentially exceeding $200,000 per year.

It's important to note that these figures are approximate and can vary significantly based on location and other factors. Successful life coaches often combine one-on-one coaching with group coaching, workshops, and other revenue streams to maximize their income.

Pursuing a career in life coaching can be deeply rewarding, both personally and professionally. It allows you to make a positive impact on others' lives while working in a field that aligns with your passion. While the road to success may have its challenges, with dedication, continuous learning, and effective marketing, you can build a thriving life coaching practice. Ultimately, the pay range in life coaching reflects the value you provide to your clients and the effort you invest in growing your coaching business.

HOME INSPECTION

Exploring the World of Home Inspection: Opportunities and Pay Range

Home inspection is a critical step in the real estate transaction process. It involves a comprehensive evaluation of a property's condition, identifying potential issues and providing valuable insights to buyers, sellers, and real estate professionals. If you have a keen eye for detail and an interest in real estate, a career in home inspection might be a fulfilling path for you. In this guide, we'll explore the steps to become a home inspector, the various aspects of the profession, potential challenges, and the pay range you can expect in this field.

Steps to Become a Home Inspector

Education and Training: Start by acquiring the necessary education and training. Many states require aspiring home inspectors to complete a formal training program. You can often find accredited courses through community colleges or specialized training schools.

Licensing and Certification: Research your state's requirements for home inspector licensing and certification. Some states have specific licensing boards or agencies responsible for regulating the profession.

Field Experience: Gain hands-on experience by working with an experienced home inspector. Many states have requirements for the number of inspections you must complete under supervision to become licensed.

Insurance and Business Setup: Establish your home inspection business, including obtaining liability insurance and any required business licenses or permits.

Tools and Equipment: Invest in the necessary tools and equipment, such as a moisture meter, infrared camera, and other inspection tools.

Marketing and Networking: Create a marketing plan to promote your services, including building a professional website, networking with real estate agents, and establishing a presence on social media platforms.

Continuing Education: Stay current in the field by participating in ongoing training and education. This is crucial to maintain your certification and keep up with industry developments.

Aspects of the Home Inspection Profession

Home inspectors provide a valuable service by evaluating various aspects of a property, including:

Structural Integrity: Assessing the condition of the foundation, walls, roof, and other structural components.

Electrical Systems: Checking the electrical wiring, outlets, and circuitry for safety and functionality.

Plumbing: Evaluating the plumbing system, including pipes, fixtures, and water heaters.

HVAC Systems: Inspecting heating, ventilation, and air conditioning systems to ensure they are in working order.

Interior and Exterior: Examining the interior and exterior of the property for issues like leaks, mold, and damage.

Safety Concerns: Identifying potential safety hazards, such as faulty wiring, radon gas, or carbon monoxide leaks.

Challenges and Considerations

The field of home inspection comes with its own set of challenges:

Licensing Requirements: Licensing requirements vary by state, and it can be time-consuming to meet all the prerequisites.

Irregular Schedule: Home inspections often occur on evenings and weekends to accommodate clients' schedules.

Client Expectations: Clients may have high expectations and can be emotionally invested in the inspection outcome, making effective communication essential.

Physical Demands: The job can be physically demanding, requiring you to climb ladders, crawl into tight spaces, and endure various weather conditions.

Competitive Market: Competition among home inspectors can be fierce, particularly in densely populated areas.

Pay Range in Home Inspection

The pay range for home inspectors varies based on factors such as location, experience, specialization, and the demand for home inspections in the area. As of my last knowledge update in September 2021, here's a general overview of the potential pay range for home inspectors:

Entry-Level Inspectors: In the early stages of your career, you may earn between $30,000 to $50,000 per year.

Experienced Inspectors: With several years of experience and a strong client base, experienced home inspectors can earn between $50,000 to $80,000 or more annually.

Specialized or Certified Inspectors: Home inspectors who specialize in areas like commercial properties, historic homes, or energy efficiency may command higher fees.

It's important to note that these figures are approximate and can vary significantly by region. Additionally, the demand for home inspections can fluctuate with the housing market. As the real estate market evolves, so do the opportunities and earning potential in the home inspection field.

A career in home inspection offers the opportunity to combine a passion for real estate with a keen eye for detail. While it comes with its challenges, the profession provides a valuable service to clients and plays a crucial role in the real estate industry. The pay range for home inspectors reflects their expertise, experience, and ability to provide accurate assessments of properties. With dedication and commitment to excellence, a career in home inspection can be both personally rewarding and financially satisfying.

USING AI TO MAKE MONEY

Leveraging AI for Profit: Opportunities and Pay Range

Artificial Intelligence (AI) has revolutionized industries across the globe, presenting new and exciting opportunities for individuals and businesses alike to harness its potential for financial gain. AI technologies, including machine learning, natural language processing, and computer vision, have the capacity to automate tasks, analyze vast amounts of data, and improve decision-making processes. In this guide, we'll explore how you can utilize AI to make money, the various avenues available, potential challenges, and the pay range associated with AI-related roles.

Using AI to Make Money

AI in Investment and Trading: AI-driven algorithms are increasingly used in stock trading, cryptocurrency markets, and other financial sectors. Traders and investors can employ AI tools to analyze market trends, identify investment opportunities, and manage portfolios more effectively.

E-commerce and Recommendations: E-commerce platforms use AI to personalize product recommendations for customers, increasing sales and customer satisfaction. Entrepreneurs can also develop AI-powered recommendation systems for their online businesses.

Content Creation: AI can generate content, including articles, reports, and marketing materials. Content creators can use AI to automate repetitive writing tasks and produce content at scale.

Data Analysis and Insights: AI-powered data analytics tools help businesses make informed decisions by extracting valuable insights from large datasets. Professionals skilled in AI data analysis are in high demand.

Chatbots and Customer Service: AI-driven chatbots provide round-the-clock customer support, helping businesses improve customer service and reduce labor costs.

Automated Trading Bots: Traders can create and deploy AI-based trading bots to execute buy and sell orders automatically, taking advantage of market fluctuations.

AI Consulting and Development Services: Offer AI consulting and development services to businesses looking to implement AI solutions. This can include developing custom AI models or integrating AI into existing systems.

Challenges and Considerations

While AI presents numerous opportunities to make money, it also comes with challenges:

Technical Expertise: Developing and deploying AI solutions requires a strong understanding of AI technologies and programming languages like Python.

Data Privacy and Security: Handling sensitive data and ensuring data privacy and security are paramount concerns when using AI.

Market Competition: The AI industry is competitive, and staying updated with the latest advancements is crucial.

Regulatory Compliance: AI applications may be subject to regulatory requirements in certain industries, such as healthcare or finance.

Pay Range in AI-Related Roles

The pay range for AI-related roles can vary significantly based on factors such as location, experience, education, and the specific job function. Here's a general overview of the potential pay range for some common AI-related roles:

AI Engineers/Developers: Entry-level AI engineers can earn between $60,000 to $100,000 annually, while experienced professionals with specialized skills can command salaries exceeding $150,000 or more.

Data Scientists: Data scientists, who often work on AI projects, can earn between $80,000 to $130,000 for entry-level positions and over $150,000 for experienced roles.

AI Consultants: AI consultants, who offer expertise to businesses, may earn between $80,000 to $150,000 or more, depending on their experience and client base.

AI Researchers: Academic or industry-based AI researchers with advanced degrees and specialized knowledge may command salaries above $150,000, particularly in research-focused roles.

It's important to note that these figures are approximate and can vary based on factors such as the specific industry, the demand for AI talent in your region, and your level of expertise. The field of AI is dynamic, and compensation can change as the industry evolves.

Leveraging AI to make money is an exciting and rapidly evolving field with numerous opportunities for innovation and financial success. As AI technologies continue to advance, individuals and businesses can capitalize on the benefits of automation, data analysis, and improved decision-making. However, success in the AI domain requires dedication, ongoing learning, and a keen understanding of the technology's capabilities and limitations. With the right skills and mindset, AI can be a powerful tool for financial growth and innovation in the modern world.

START A PHOTO BOTH COMPANY

A Snapshot of Success: Starting a Photo Booth Rental Business

Photo booth rental businesses have become a popular and profitable venture in recent years. These portable, fun-filled spaces offer event attendees a chance to capture memorable moments, and they've become a staple at weddings, parties, corporate events, and more. If you're considering entering this exciting industry, this guide will provide insights into starting a photo booth rental business, the key aspects to consider, potential challenges, and the pay range you can expect.

Starting a Photo Booth Rental Business

Market Research: Begin by conducting thorough market research to understand the demand for photo booth rentals in your area. Identify your target audience, competitors, and potential niches within the market.

Business Plan: Develop a comprehensive business plan that outlines your business goals, target market, pricing strategy, marketing plan, and financial projections. A well-crafted plan is essential for securing funding and staying on track.

Equipment and Setup: Invest in high-quality photo booth equipment, including cameras, lighting, backdrops, props, and printing technology. Ensure your setup is user-friendly and provides excellent image quality.

Legal Requirements: Register your business, obtain any necessary permits or licenses, and secure liability insurance to protect your business and clients.

Website and Online Presence: Create a professional website showcasing your photo booth options, packages, and galleries of past events. An active online presence can help attract customers.

Marketing and Promotion: Develop marketing strategies to promote your services, which may include social media advertising, networking with event planners, and offering special promotions for bookings.

Event Booking and Customer Service: Streamline the booking process and provide excellent customer service to clients. Timely communication and reliability are key to building a positive reputation.

Challenges and Considerations

Running a successful photo booth rental business comes with its share of challenges:

Competition: The photo booth rental industry is competitive, and differentiating your services is crucial to stand out.

Equipment Maintenance: Regular maintenance of your equipment is essential to ensure that it operates smoothly at events.

Transportation and Setup: Transporting and setting up photo booths can be physically demanding, especially for larger events.

Seasonal Demand: Demand for photo booth rentals may vary seasonally, with more bookings during peak event seasons.

Client Expectations: Clients often have high expectations for their events, so delivering a seamless and enjoyable photo booth experience is essential.

Pay Range in Photo Booth Rental

The pay range in the photo booth rental industry varies based on factors such as location, the types of events you cater to, the quality of your equipment, and the packages you offer. Here's a general estimate of the potential pay range for photo booth rental business owners:

Startup Phase (First Year): In the initial stages, business owners may earn between $20,000 to $40,000 annually, depending on the number of events booked.

Growth Phase (2-5 Years): With successful marketing efforts and a growing client base, annual earnings can range from $40,000 to $80,000 or more.

Established Business (5+ Years): Established photo booth rental companies with a strong reputation can earn annual revenues exceeding $100,000 or more.

It's important to note that these figures are approximate and can vary significantly based on your location and business strategies. The key to financial success in the photo booth rental industry is delivering exceptional service, marketing effectively, and building lasting relationships with clients and event planners.

Starting a photo booth rental business can be a rewarding endeavor, offering opportunities to be a part of special events and celebrations while earning a living. However, success in this industry requires careful planning, attention to detail, and dedication to providing top-notch service. By differentiating your business, effectively marketing your services, and consistently delivering a memorable photo booth experience, you can build a thriving business with a satisfying pay range in this exciting niche.

START A MOBILE
CAR WASHING COMPANY

Clean Profits: Starting a Mobile Car Wash Business

Mobile car wash businesses have gained popularity in recent years, offering convenience and eco-friendly services to vehicle owners. This entrepreneurial venture provides an excellent opportunity for individuals looking to start their own business. In this guide, we will explore the steps to establish a mobile car wash business, essential considerations, potential challenges, and the pay range you can expect in this industry.

Starting a Mobile Car Wash Business

Market Research: Begin by conducting thorough market research to identify the demand for mobile car wash services in your area. Understand your target audience and assess the competition.

Business Plan: Develop a comprehensive business plan outlining your business goals, service offerings, pricing strategy, marketing plan, and financial projections. A well-structured plan will guide your business growth.

Legal Requirements: Register your business and ensure compliance with local regulations and environmental standards. Obtain any necessary permits or licenses.

Equipment and Supplies: Invest in high-quality cleaning equipment, water tanks, cleaning solutions, and detailing tools. Choose eco-friendly products to appeal to environmentally-conscious customers.

Vehicle Preparation: Equip your mobile car wash vehicle with the necessary storage, water supply, and power sources. Ensure it is well-maintained and showcases your professionalism.

Branding and Marketing: Create a strong brand identity, including a memorable logo and marketing materials. Develop a professional website and establish an online presence through social media to attract customers.

Pricing and Packages: Determine your pricing structure and service packages. Offer competitive rates while ensuring you cover your operating costs and generate profit.

Client Acquisition: Develop marketing strategies to attract clients, such as offering first-time customer discounts, partnering with local businesses, and utilizing customer referrals.

Challenges and Considerations

Running a mobile car wash business comes with its set of challenges:

Weather Dependency: Weather conditions can affect business operations, especially if you operate in an area with extreme climates. Plan for seasonal variations.

Water and Environmental Regulations: Be aware of local regulations regarding water usage and disposal. Implement environmentally-friendly practices to reduce your carbon footprint.

Equipment Maintenance: Regular maintenance and repairs of your cleaning equipment are necessary to ensure efficient operations.

Customer Scheduling: Managing customer appointments and ensuring timely arrivals at different locations can be challenging.

Competition: The mobile car wash industry is competitive, so differentiating your services and maintaining high-quality standards is essential.

Pay Range in Mobile Car Wash

The pay range for mobile car wash businesses can vary widely based on factors such as location, the number of clients served, pricing strategy, and the quality of services provided. Here's a general estimate of the potential pay range for mobile car wash business owners:

Startup Phase (First Year): In the initial stages, business owners may earn between $20,000 to $40,000 annually, depending on the number of clients served.

Growth Phase (2-5 Years): With effective marketing and a growing client base, annual earnings can range from $40,000 to $80,000 or more.

Established Business (5+ Years): Well-established mobile car wash businesses with a loyal customer base can earn annual revenues exceeding $100,000 or more.

It's important to note that these figures are approximate and can vary significantly based on your location, pricing strategy, and business performance. Success in the mobile car wash industry hinges on providing top-quality service, effectively marketing your business, and building long-term relationships with clients. Additionally, offering additional services like interior detailing or specialized treatments can increase your income potential.

Starting a mobile car wash business can be a rewarding journey, offering the freedom of entrepreneurship while providing a valuable service to vehicle owners. With careful planning, effective marketing, and a commitment to excellence, you can build a thriving business with a satisfying pay range in the mobile car wash industry. As customer satisfaction and word-of-mouth referrals grow, so will your business and financial success.

START A VIDEOGRAPHY BUSINESS

Starting a Videography Business: Capturing Moments and Profits

Videography is an artful and dynamic profession that allows you to tell stories, capture moments, and create lasting memories through the lens of a camera. If you have a passion for visual storytelling and want to turn your skills into a profitable venture, starting a videography business can be a fulfilling and financially rewarding path. In this guide, we'll explore the steps to establish a videography business, key considerations, potential challenges, and the pay range you can expect in this creative industry.

Steps to Launching a Videography Business

Starting a videography business involves a series of strategic steps:

Skills and Equipment: Begin by honing your videography skills and investing in high-quality equipment. Your toolkit may include cameras, lenses, tripods, stabilizers, lighting, audio recording tools, and editing software.

Legal Structure: Choose a legal structure for your business, such as a sole proprietorship, LLC (Limited Liability Company), or corporation. Register your business with the appropriate authorities and obtain any necessary licenses or permits.

Portfolio Development: Build a compelling portfolio showcasing your work. Include a variety of projects to demonstrate your versatility, such as weddings, events, corporate videos, documentaries, or promotional content.

Business Plan: Develop a comprehensive business plan outlining your goals, target market, pricing strategy, marketing plan, and financial projections. A well-structured plan will guide your business growth and help secure financing if needed.

Branding and Marketing: Create a strong brand identity, including a memorable logo and marketing materials. Build an online presence through a professional website, social media platforms, and online portfolios to attract potential clients.

Client Acquisition: Develop marketing strategies to attract clients, such as offering introductory rates, partnering with event planners, and leveraging word-of-mouth referrals. Networking within your local community and industry can also be valuable.

Challenges and Considerations

Running a successful videography business comes with its set of challenges:

Competition: The videography industry is competitive, with many talented professionals vying for clients. Differentiating your services and style is crucial.

Client Expectations: Clients often have high expectations for their projects, so clear communication, meeting deadlines, and delivering exceptional work are essential to building a positive reputation.

Equipment Maintenance: Regular maintenance and updating of your equipment are necessary to ensure the quality of your work.

Unpredictable Income: Income in the videography business can be unpredictable, with busy and slow seasons. Effective financial management is essential.

Legal and Contractual Matters: Familiarize yourself with contract laws, intellectual property rights, and licensing agreements to protect your work and business interests.

Pay Range in Videography

The pay range in the videography industry varies widely based on factors such as location, niche specialization, experience, the complexity of projects, and client budgets. Here's a general estimate of the potential pay range for videographers:

Entry-Level Videographers: In the early stages of your career, you may earn between $30,000 to $60,000 per year, depending on your location and the number of projects you secure.

Experienced Videographers: With several years of experience, annual earnings can range from $60,000 to $100,000 or more. Experienced professionals who specialize in specific niches or high-end markets may command higher rates.

Corporate or Commercial Videographers: Videographers who focus on corporate or commercial projects may have higher earning potential, with some earning six-figure incomes, especially in major metropolitan areas.

It's important to note that these figures are approximate and can vary significantly based on your location and the demand for videography services in your area. Successful videographers often increase their income potential by offering additional services, such as video editing, drone footage, or specialized post-production work.

Starting a videography business offers the opportunity to turn your creative passion into a profitable profession. While the industry can be competitive and comes with its challenges, it also provides a platform to capture meaningful moments, tell compelling stories, and build a thriving business. Success in videography depends on your skills, dedication, and ability to deliver exceptional work that resonates with clients and viewers. As your reputation grows, so will your earning potential in this dynamic and visually captivating field.

DRIVING FOR A

RIDE -SHARING SERVICE

Hitting the Road for Profit: Driving for a Ride-Sharing Service

In recent years, ride-sharing services like Uber and Lyft have revolutionized the way people commute and travel, while also providing flexible income opportunities for drivers. If you're interested in becoming a ride-sharing driver, this guide will walk you through the process, key considerations, potential challenges, and the pay range you can expect in this fast-growing industry.

Becoming a Ride-Sharing Driver

Starting a career as a ride-sharing driver is relatively straightforward, but it does require some essential steps:

Meet the Requirements: Ensure you meet the minimum requirements set by the ride-sharing company of your choice. These typically include age restrictions, vehicle specifications, and a valid driver's license.

Vehicle Selection: If you meet the requirements, choose a vehicle that meets the ride-sharing company's standards. It should be in good condition, comfortable for passengers, and meet any age or model requirements.

Background Check: Be prepared to undergo a background check. Ride-sharing companies prioritize passenger safety and will typically assess your driving history and criminal record.

Insurance: Verify your auto insurance coverage. Ride-sharing companies often require drivers to have appropriate insurance, and some offer additional coverage while you're driving for the platform.

App Sign-Up: Download the ride-sharing company's driver app, create an account, and complete the registration process. This may include providing documentation and vehicle details.

Vehicle Inspection: Schedule and pass a vehicle inspection, which is typically done at an approved inspection center.

Orientation: Some ride-sharing companies offer in-person or online orientation sessions to familiarize you with their platform and policies.

Hit the Road: Once approved, you're ready to start accepting ride requests and earning money as a ride-sharing driver.

Challenges and Considerations

While driving for a ride-sharing service can be a flexible and lucrative gig, it comes with its share of challenges:

Income Variability: Ride-sharing income can vary greatly depending on factors like location, time of day, and demand. Earnings may not always be consistent.

Expenses: Drivers are responsible for their vehicle's maintenance, fuel, and other operating costs. It's important to factor these expenses into your financial planning.

Long Hours: Some drivers work long hours to maximize their earnings, which can be physically and mentally demanding.

Customer Service: Dealing with various passengers, each with their own expectations and needs, requires excellent customer service skills and patience.

Safety Concerns: Driving late at night or in unfamiliar areas can pose safety risks. Ride-sharing companies provide safety features, but drivers should remain vigilant.

Pay Range for Ride-Sharing Drivers

The pay range for ride-sharing drivers can vary widely based on several factors:

Location: Earnings often depend on your city or region. Larger cities with higher demand may offer higher fares and more frequent rides.

Time of Day: Peak hours, such as rush hour or weekends, tend to yield higher earnings due to increased demand.

Number of Rides: Earnings are directly correlated with the number of rides you complete. Drivers who work more hours and accept more rides generally earn more.

Tips and Bonuses: Tips and bonuses from passengers can significantly boost your income.

The approximate pay range for ride-sharing drivers in the United States was:

Base Earnings: Ride-sharing drivers earned an average of $15 to $25 per hour before expenses.

Additional Earnings: Tips, bonuses, and surge pricing during high-demand times could add significantly to your income.

It's important to note that these figures are approximate and can vary based on your location, the ride-sharing company you drive for, and market conditions. To maximize your earnings, it's essential to understand the local market, drive during peak hours, and provide excellent customer service.

Driving for a ride-sharing service can be a flexible and potentially lucrative way to earn income while having the freedom to set your own schedule. While it comes with challenges and uncertainties, many individuals find it to be a rewarding and financially viable gig. Whether you're looking to supplement your income or make ride-sharing a full-time career, success as a ride-sharing driver depends on factors like location, time commitment, and a commitment to providing excellent service to passengers.

START A PODCAST

Embark on Your Podcasting Journey: Sharing Your Passion and Earning Potential

Podcasting has evolved into a powerful medium that enables creators to connect with audiences worldwide, share their passions, and even generate income. If you're considering starting your own podcast, this guide will take you through the process, key considerations, potential challenges, and the pay range you can anticipate in the realm of podcasting.

Getting Started in Podcasting

Launching your podcast entails a series of key steps:

Find Your Niche: Choose a subject or theme that you're passionate about and that resonates with your target audience. Identifying a niche can help you stand out in the competitive podcasting landscape.

Content Planning: Outline your episodes, plan your content, and decide on your podcast's format. Will it be a solo show, an interview-style podcast, or a collaborative effort with co-hosts?

Acquire Recording Equipment: Invest in quality audio recording equipment, including a microphone, headphones, and audio editing software. Excellent audio quality is vital for retaining and expanding your listener base.

Recording and Editing: Record and edit your episodes meticulously to ensure they are engaging and free from technical issues. Pay attention to sound quality, pacing, and storytelling.

Hosting and Distribution: Choose a podcast hosting platform to store and distribute your episodes to major podcast directories such as Apple Podcasts, Spotify, and Google Podcasts.

Branding and Promotion: Create podcast artwork and branding materials to make your show visually appealing. Promote your podcast through social media, your website, and other marketing channels.

Engage with Your Audience: Actively interact with your audience through social media, emails, and listener feedback. Building a community around your podcast can lead to loyal listeners.

Challenges and Considerations

While podcasting can be a highly rewarding endeavor, it also comes with its set of challenges:

Consistency: Maintaining a regular podcasting schedule can be challenging but is crucial for building and retaining your audience.

Quality Control: Ensuring high audio quality, content relevance, and engaging storytelling requires continuous effort and improvement.

Promotion: Standing out in the crowded podcasting space can be difficult. Effective marketing and promotion are essential for growing your audience.

Monetization: While there are various ways to monetize your podcast, generating significant revenue may take time and effort.

Time and Resource Investment: Podcasting can be time-consuming, especially when it comes to content creation, editing, and promotion.

Pay Range in Podcasting

Earning potential in podcasting varies widely and depends on several factors:

Advertising Revenue: Many podcasters monetize their shows through advertising. Rates can range from a few dollars per thousand downloads (CPM) to significantly higher rates for popular shows with large audiences.

Sponsorships: Podcasters can secure sponsorships from companies or brands in their niche. Sponsorship deals can range from a few hundred dollars to several thousand dollars per episode, depending on audience size and niche relevance.

Donations and Crowdfunding: Some podcasters rely on listener donations or crowdfunding platforms like Patreon to support their shows.

Merchandise Sales: Selling merchandise related to your podcast, such as t-shirts or mugs, can provide an additional revenue stream.

Popular podcasts with substantial audiences could earn significant revenue, sometimes reaching six or seven figures annually. However, it's important to note that the vast majority of podcasts generate modest income or operate as passion projects.

Popular Podcasts

Here are a few examples of popular podcasts across various genres, showcasing the diversity of content in the medium:

"The Joe Rogan Experience": Hosted by comedian Joe Rogan, this long-form podcast features in-depth conversations with a wide range of guests, from scientists to celebrities.

"Serial": Known for its investigative journalism, "Serial" delves into true crime stories, exploring one case per season.

"The Daily": A news and analysis podcast by The New York Times, "The Daily" provides in-depth coverage of current events and stories shaping the world.

"How I Built This": Host Guy Raz interviews entrepreneurs and innovators, diving into the stories behind successful companies and products.

"Science Vs": This podcast takes a scientific approach to debunking myths and exploring controversial topics, from diets to essential oils.

These podcasts represent just a small sample of the diverse content available in the podcasting world. They also illustrate the potential for success and financial viability in the medium, as many popular podcasters have built substantial audiences and monetized their shows effectively.

Podcasting offers a unique platform for individuals to share their voices, stories, and expertise with a global audience. While it comes with challenges, those who are passionate about their topics and committed to creating quality content can find success in podcasting. Whether you're aiming to make podcasting your full-time career or a side hustle, the potential for financial rewards is there, especially as your audience grows and you explore various monetization avenues.

DELIVERING GROCERIES

Delivering Convenience and Earning Income: A Guide to Food and Grocery Delivery

In recent years, the gig economy has opened up numerous opportunities for individuals to earn income by delivering food, groceries, and other essentials through platforms like Uber Eats, Instacart, and DoorDash. If you're considering entering this field, this guide will provide you with insights into the process, key considerations, potential challenges, and the pay range you can expect when delivering for these services.

Becoming a Delivery Driver

Starting a career as a food or grocery delivery driver is accessible and typically involves these steps:

Meet the Requirements: Ensure you meet the minimum requirements set by the delivery platform you intend to work with. These typically include age restrictions, a valid driver's license, and a reliable mode of transportation.

App Installation: Download the app of the delivery platform you plan to work for and complete the registration process. You'll likely need to provide personal information and pass a background check.

Vehicle and Equipment: Depending on the platform, you may use your car, a bicycle, or even walk for deliveries. Make sure your vehicle is in good condition, or if you're delivering groceries, have access to a shopping cart.

Choose Your Schedule: Delivery platforms offer flexible schedules, allowing you to work when it's convenient for you. You can set your own hours and decide how much or how little you want to work.

Accepting Orders: Once you're approved, you can start accepting delivery orders through the app. You'll receive information about the order, the delivery location, and any special instructions.

Complete Deliveries: Pick up the food or groceries from the designated location and deliver them to the customer's doorstep. Ensure timely and accurate deliveries to maintain a good rating.

Challenges and Considerations

While working as a food or grocery delivery driver can offer flexibility and earning potential, it's essential to be aware of the following challenges:

Income Variability: Earnings can fluctuate based on factors like location, time of day, and the number of deliveries you complete. Income may not always be consistent.

Expenses: Drivers are responsible for vehicle maintenance, fuel costs, and other operational expenses. It's crucial to factor these expenses into your financial planning.

Long Hours: Some drivers work long hours to maximize their earnings, which can be physically and mentally demanding.

Customer Service: Dealing with various customers, each with their own expectations and needs, requires excellent customer service skills and patience.

Safety Concerns: Driving in unfamiliar areas or late at night can pose safety risks. Delivery platforms often provide safety features, but drivers should remain vigilant.

Pay Range in Food and Grocery Delivery

The pay range for food and grocery delivery drivers can vary based on several factors:

Location: Earnings depend significantly on your city or region. Larger cities with higher demand may offer higher delivery fees and more frequent orders.

Time of Day: Peak hours, such as lunch and dinner times, tend to yield higher earnings due to increased demand.

Number of Deliveries: Earnings are directly correlated with the number of deliveries you complete. Drivers who work more hours and accept more orders generally earn more.

Tips: Tips from customers can significantly boost your income. Providing excellent service and maintaining a high rating can lead to more generous tips.

Bonuses: Some delivery platforms offer bonuses for completing a certain number of deliveries within a specified time frame.

Food and grocery delivery drivers in the United States typically earned an average of $10 to $20 per hour before expenses, with the potential to earn more during peak times and with tips. However, these figures can vary widely depending on location and individual performance.

Delivering food and groceries through platforms like Uber Eats, Instacart, and DoorDash can be a flexible and convenient way to earn income. While it offers advantages like setting your own schedule, it also comes with challenges and uncertainties. Success in this field depends on factors such as location, time commitment, and customer service skills. As you gain experience and build a reputation for reliable and efficient delivery, you can increase your earning potential in this growing gig economy sector.

TWITCH STREAMING

Level Up Your Streaming Game: A Guide to Twitch Streaming

Twitch, the leading live streaming platform, has opened up exciting opportunities for individuals to turn their hobbies and passions into income-generating careers. If you're considering diving into the world of Twitch streaming, this guide will provide you with insights into the process, key considerations, potential challenges, and the pay range you can expect as a Twitch streamer.

Getting Started with Twitch Streaming

Starting a career as a Twitch streamer involves several key steps:

Choose Your Niche: Identify your area of interest or expertise. Whether it's gaming, cooking, music, art, or any other passion, Twitch has a diverse audience for various niches.

Create a Twitch Account: If you don't have one already, sign up for a Twitch account. Choose a memorable username, complete your profile, and upload a profile picture and banner.

Set Up Your Streaming Equipment: Invest in the necessary streaming equipment, including a computer with sufficient processing power, a high-quality microphone, a webcam, and streaming software like OBS Studio.

Design Your Stream: Customize your stream layout, including overlays, alerts, and chat bots. Create a visually appealing and engaging stream to attract viewers.

Establish a Streaming Schedule: Consistency is key to building an audience. Establish a regular streaming schedule and stick to it. Inform your viewers about your streaming times.

Engage with Your Audience: Interact with your viewers through live chat. Engaging with your audience, responding to questions, and fostering a sense of community can help grow your channel.

Monetization: As your channel grows, explore monetization options, such as subscriptions, donations, and sponsorships.

Challenges and Considerations

Streaming on Twitch can be highly rewarding, but it's essential to be aware of the following challenges:

Competition: Twitch is a competitive platform with millions of streamers. Standing out and building an audience can be challenging.

Consistency: Maintaining a regular streaming schedule can be demanding, and taking breaks can result in a loss of viewers.

Monetization: Building a sustainable income on Twitch may take time. Reliance on income from subscriptions, donations, and sponsorships can be unpredictable.

Quality Control: Ensuring high-quality audio and video, as well as a stable stream, requires ongoing effort and investment in equipment.

Content Variety: While sticking to your niche is important, offering variety within your chosen category can help keep viewers engaged.

Pay Range in Twitch Streaming

The pay range for Twitch streamers can vary widely based on several factors:

Audience Size: The number of followers and concurrent viewers you have significantly impacts your income potential. Streamers with larger audiences can earn more from subscriptions, donations, and ads.

Subscriptions: Twitch offers a subscription model where viewers can pay a monthly fee to access exclusive content and support their favorite streamers. Streamers typically receive a percentage of the subscription revenue.

Donations: Viewers can donate directly to streamers during their broadcasts. The amount of donations can vary greatly but can be a significant source of income for popular streamers.

Ad Revenue: Streamers can earn money from ads shown during their streams. Ad revenue is influenced by the number of viewers and ad completion rates.

Sponsorship and Brand Deals: As your channel grows, you may attract sponsorships and brand deals, where companies pay you to promote their products or services.

Merchandise Sales: Some streamers create and sell merchandise related to their channel, which can provide additional income.

Twitch streamers could earn anywhere from a few hundred dollars per month to several thousand dollars per month or more, depending on their audience size, engagement, and monetization strategies. Popular streamers with tens of thousands of viewers could potentially earn a substantial income.

Twitch streaming offers an exciting avenue to turn your passions into a career. While it comes with challenges and uncertainties, those who are dedicated, consistent, and engaging can find success on the platform. Building an audience and monetizing your channel may take time, but as your community grows, so does your potential for income. Whether you aim to make streaming a full-time career or a side hustle, Twitch provides an accessible and rewarding platform to share your passions and entertain a global audience.

MOBILE PHONE REPAIR BUSINESS

Launching a Lucrative Venture: Starting a Mobile Phone Repair Business

In today's tech-driven world, mobile phones have become an integral part of our lives. With the growing number of smartphones, there's a significant demand for mobile phone repair services. If you're tech-savvy and considering starting your own mobile phone repair business, this guide will provide you with insights into the process, key considerations, potential challenges, and the pay range you can expect in this thriving industry.

Steps to Launching a Mobile Phone Repair Business

Starting a mobile phone repair business involves a series of strategic steps:

Acquire the Necessary Skills: To succeed in this industry, you'll need a strong understanding of mobile phone hardware and software. Consider enrolling in courses or certifications related to mobile phone repair.

Create a Business Plan: Develop a comprehensive business plan outlining your goals, target market, pricing strategy, startup costs, and financial projections. A well-structured plan will guide your business growth and help secure financing if needed.

Legal and Business Structure: Choose a legal structure for your business, such as a sole proprietorship, LLC (Limited Liability Company), or corporation. Register your business with the appropriate authorities and obtain any necessary licenses or permits.

Location and Equipment: Set up a dedicated workspace for your repair operations. Invest in quality tools and equipment needed for mobile phone repairs, including screwdrivers, soldering equipment, and diagnostic tools.

Supplier Relationships: Establish relationships with suppliers to source genuine replacement parts and accessories. Reliable suppliers are essential to ensure the quality of your repairs.

Marketing and Branding: Create a strong brand identity for your business, including a memorable logo and marketing materials. Build an online presence through a professional website and social media to attract potential customers.

Services and Pricing: Determine the range of services you will offer, such as screen replacements, battery replacements, and software troubleshooting. Set competitive pricing while ensuring profitability.

Customer Service: Excellent customer service and transparent communication are vital to building trust with your clients.

Challenges and Considerations

Running a successful mobile phone repair business comes with its set of challenges:

Technical Updates: The mobile phone industry is constantly evolving, with new models and technologies. Staying up-to-date with the latest repairs and techniques is essential.

Competition: The repair industry can be competitive, so differentiating your services and providing exceptional quality and customer service are crucial.

Parts and Inventory Management: Managing inventory and ensuring a consistent supply of replacement parts can be challenging.

Data Privacy: Handling customer data and ensuring data privacy and security are essential in this business.

Marketing and Promotion: Effective marketing and promotion are crucial to stand out in the market and attract customers.

Pay Range in Mobile Phone Repair

The pay range for mobile phone repair technicians can vary based on factors such as location, experience, expertise, and the types of repairs offered. As of my last knowledge update in September 2021, here's a general estimate of the potential pay range:

Entry-Level Technicians: In the early stages of your career, you may earn an hourly wage ranging from $10 to $20 per hour, depending on your location and the complexity of repairs.

Experienced Technicians: With several years of experience and expertise in advanced repairs, you can earn between $20 to $40 or more per hour. Some technicians with specialized skills may command higher rates.

Business Owners: As the owner of a mobile phone repair business, your income potential can be significant. Profitability depends on factors such as the number of repairs, pricing, and operating costs.

It's important to note that these figures are approximate and can vary significantly based on your location and the demand for mobile phone repair services in your area. Success in this business often involves offering high-quality repairs, outstanding customer service, and efficient operations.

Starting a mobile phone repair business is a viable and potentially profitable venture, especially in today's smartphone-centric world. Success in this industry hinges on your technical skills, business acumen, and commitment to providing reliable and efficient repair services. As you build a reputation for quality work and customer satisfaction, your mobile phone repair business can become a trusted resource in your community, offering you the potential for long-term success and financial stability.

SELLING ONLINE COURSES

Creating and Selling Online Courses: A Guide to Sharing Your Expertise

In today's digital age, the demand for online education is on the rise. If you possess knowledge or expertise in a particular subject and are interested in sharing it with a global audience, creating and selling online courses can be a rewarding endeavor. This guide will take you through the process, key considerations, potential challenges, and the pay range associated with developing and selling online courses.

Steps to Create and Sell Online Courses

1. Identify Your Expertise:

Determine your area of expertise or the subject you're passionate about.

Assess the demand for courses in your chosen field.

2. Define Your Target Audience:

Identify your ideal learners. Consider their backgrounds, needs, and skill levels.

Tailor your course content to meet the specific requirements of your target audience.

3. Course Planning:

Outline your course structure, including modules, lessons, and assessments.

Create a detailed course syllabus and learning objectives.

4. Content Creation:

Develop engaging course materials, such as video lectures, written content, quizzes, and assignments.

Ensure your content is well-organized, easy to understand, and of high quality.

5. Choose a Platform:

Select an online course platform or learning management system (LMS) to host your courses.

Popular platforms include Udemy, Coursera, Teachable, and Thinkific.

6. Create a Sales and Marketing Strategy:

Develop a marketing plan to promote your courses.

Consider using social media, email marketing, and content marketing to reach potential students.

7. Pricing and Monetization:

Determine your course pricing strategy. Factors to consider include course length, depth, and market competition.

Explore different monetization models, such as one-time payments, subscriptions, or tiered pricing.

8. Launch and Support:

Launch your course, and provide ongoing support to your students through discussion boards, email, or live Q&A sessions.

Collect and act on feedback to improve your courses continuously.

Challenges and Considerations

Creating and selling online courses can be a rewarding endeavor, but it comes with its set of challenges:

Content Quality: Ensuring that your course content is engaging, informative, and well-structured is essential to attracting and retaining students.

Marketing: Successfully promoting your courses and standing out in a crowded online education marketplace can be challenging.

Competition: The online course market is highly competitive. It's crucial to differentiate your offerings and build a strong brand.

Technical Proficiency: Familiarity with online course platforms and technical tools is necessary for creating and managing your courses.

Pay Range for Online Course Creators

The pay range for online course creators can vary widely depending on several factors:

Course Quality: High-quality, in-depth courses often command higher prices and generate more revenue.

Marketing and Promotion: Effective marketing efforts can lead to more course enrollments and increased income.

Niche or Subject: Courses in specialized or in-demand fields may generate higher revenue.

Pricing Model: Your chosen pricing model, such as one-time payments, subscriptions, or tiered pricing, affects your income potential.

Course Popularity: Popular courses with a large number of enrolled students can generate significant income.

Online course creators could earn anywhere from a few hundred to several thousand dollars per month, depending on the factors mentioned above. Exceptional courses with a substantial student base can even generate substantial income.

Creating and selling online courses can be a fulfilling way to share your expertise, help others learn, and generate income from your knowledge. While it requires careful planning, content creation, marketing efforts, and ongoing support, the potential for financial rewards and personal satisfaction makes it an attractive option for educators, experts, and entrepreneurs. By delivering high-quality courses tailored to your audience's needs, you can establish yourself as a valuable resource in the world of online education.

SELLING ARTISAN

PRODUCTS

Crafting Success: A Guide to Selling Artisan Products

In a world driven by mass production, artisan products have gained a special place in the hearts of consumers who appreciate quality, craftsmanship, and unique items. If you're a skilled artisan looking to turn your craft into a business, this guide will walk you through the process, key considerations, potential challenges, and the pay range associated with selling artisan products.

Steps to Selling Artisan Products

1. Define Your Niche:

Identify the type of artisan products you want to create and sell. This could include handmade jewelry, ceramics, textiles, candles, woodworking, or any other craft.

2. Hone Your Craft:

Continuously improve your skills and craftsmanship. Quality is paramount in the artisan market.

3. Create Your Inventory:

Develop a diverse range of products within your niche. Offer various designs, styles, and price points to cater to a wider audience.

4. Set Prices:

Determine pricing that covers your production costs, includes a profit margin, and remains competitive in the market. Consider factors like materials, labor, and overhead.

5. Choose Sales Channels:

Decide where you will sell your artisan products. Options include online marketplaces (Etsy, Amazon Handmade), craft fairs, local boutiques, and your own website.

6. Marketing and Branding:

Develop a strong brand identity that reflects your craft's unique selling points.

Utilize online and offline marketing strategies, including social media, email marketing, and collaborations with influencers or local businesses.

7. Inventory Management:

Keep track of your inventory, including materials and finished products, to ensure a smooth sales process.

8. Customer Engagement:

Foster relationships with customers through excellent customer service, personalization, and engagement. Collect feedback and use it to improve your products.

Challenges and Considerations

Selling artisan products can be a rewarding venture, but it's important to be aware of the following challenges:

Time-Intensive: Crafting artisan products can be time-consuming, and scaling production may require additional resources.

Market Saturation: Depending on your niche, you may face competition from other artisans. Effective branding and marketing can help you stand out.

Pricing: Finding the right balance between pricing your products competitively and ensuring profitability can be challenging.

Marketing: Effectively reaching your target audience and building brand recognition requires marketing efforts.

Pay Range for Selling Artisan Products

The pay range for selling artisan products varies widely depending on several factors:

Product Type: The type of artisan products you create influences your income potential. Unique, high-quality, and in-demand products often command higher prices.

Pricing Strategy: Your chosen pricing strategy, whether you sell premium or budget-friendly products, affects your revenue.

Marketing and Promotion: Effective marketing efforts can lead to more sales and increased income.

Market Demand: The demand for your artisan products within your niche or industry can impact your sales volume.

Sales Channels: Different sales channels may have varying fees or commissions, which can affect your overall income.

Artisan product sellers could earn anywhere from a few hundred to several thousand dollars per month or more, depending on the factors mentioned above. Success often depends on offering unique and high-quality products, effective marketing, and the ability to connect with customers who value craftsmanship.

Selling artisan products allows you to share your unique skills and creations with a discerning audience that appreciates craftsmanship and authenticity. While it requires dedication and effort, turning your craft into a business can be a fulfilling and profitable endeavor. By focusing on quality, effective branding, and marketing, as well as maintaining strong customer relationships, you can build a successful artisan business and turn your passion into a sustainable source of income.

RETAIL ARBITRAGE

Unlocking Profit Potential: A Guide to Retail Arbitrage

Retail arbitrage is a dynamic and increasingly popular business model that allows entrepreneurs to find products at lower prices in one market and sell them at a profit in another. If you're interested in exploring the world of retail arbitrage, this guide will provide insights into the process, key considerations, potential challenges, and the pay range associated with this entrepreneurial pursuit.

Understanding Retail Arbitrage

Retail arbitrage involves the following key steps:

1. Sourcing Products:

Research and identify products that are in demand or have potential for profit.

Find sources where you can purchase these products at a lower cost. Common sources include retail stores, clearance sales, liquidation sales, and online marketplaces.

2. Price Comparison:

Compare the prices of the sourced products with the prices they command in other markets, such as online marketplaces like Amazon or eBay.

3. Purchase and Resale:

Buy the selected products at a lower price and list them for sale in the target market, often online.

Consider factors such as shipping costs, fees, and market demand when determining your selling price.

4. Fulfillment and Customer Service:

Fulfill customer orders, handle shipping, and provide customer support as needed.

5. Continuous Sourcing:

Continuously source new products and expand your inventory to maximize profit opportunities.

Challenges and Considerations

While retail arbitrage offers the potential for profit, it comes with its set of challenges:

Market Fluctuations: Prices can change rapidly in the retail market, impacting your ability to secure products at a profit.

Competition: The retail arbitrage space is competitive, and other sellers may drive prices down, affecting your profit margins.

Inventory Management: Effective inventory management is crucial to prevent overstocking or understocking.

Platform Rules: If you choose to sell on platforms like Amazon, you'll need to adhere to their rules and guidelines.

Pay Range in Retail Arbitrage

The pay range in retail arbitrage can vary significantly based on several factors:

Product Selection: The type of products you choose to arbitrage can greatly impact your income potential. High-demand, high-margin products tend to yield higher profits.

Sourcing Skills: Your ability to find profitable sourcing opportunities and negotiate deals with suppliers is crucial.

Marketplace Choice: The marketplace or platform you use to sell your products can affect your income. Different platforms have varying fees and seller requirements.

Market Demand: The demand for the products you source plays a significant role in determining your profit potential.

Efficiency: Your ability to efficiently list, sell, and fulfill orders can impact your overall income.

Successful retail arbitrage sellers could earn anywhere from a few hundred to several thousand dollars per month or more, depending on the factors mentioned above. Exceptional sellers with a keen eye for profitable products and effective sourcing strategies can achieve significant income.

Retail arbitrage offers an entrepreneurial opportunity for individuals with a knack for spotting profitable deals and a willingness to navigate the complexities of the retail market. While it comes with challenges, those who excel in product selection, sourcing, and efficient selling can build a profitable business. Success in retail arbitrage often involves continuous learning, adaptability, and a commitment to finding and capitalizing on opportunities in the ever-changing retail landscape.

PRIVATE LABEL

Private Label Products: A Path to Entrepreneurial Success

Private label products are a thriving business model that allows entrepreneurs to create their own brands and sell products manufactured by third-party suppliers. If you're interested in exploring the world of private label products, this guide will provide insights into the process, key considerations, potential challenges, and the pay range associated with this entrepreneurial venture.

Understanding Private Label Products

Private label products involve the following key steps:

1. Product Selection:

Identify products you want to sell under your own brand. Consider factors like market demand, competition, and profit potential.

2. Supplier Sourcing:

Find reliable suppliers or manufacturers who can produce your chosen products with your branding and packaging specifications.

3. Branding and Packaging:

Develop a brand identity, including a brand name, logo, and packaging design.

Customize the product's packaging and labeling to reflect your brand.

4. Quality Control:

Ensure that the products meet your quality standards. This may involve product testing and sample inspections.

5. Marketing and Sales:

Create a marketing strategy to promote your private label products. This includes product listings, online presence, and advertising.

Establish sales channels, which may include your own e-commerce website or platforms like Amazon or Shopify.

6. Fulfillment and Customer Service:

Handle order fulfillment, shipping, and provide customer support as needed.

Challenges and Considerations

Launching a private label product business comes with its set of challenges:

Supplier Relations: Finding and maintaining strong relationships with reliable suppliers is crucial to the success of your business.

Quality Assurance: Ensuring that the products meet your quality standards is essential to maintain customer trust and satisfaction.

Competition: The market for private label products can be competitive, so effective branding and marketing are vital.

Inventory Management: Efficiently managing inventory and forecasting demand is key to preventing overstocking or understocking.

Pay Range in Private Label Products

The pay range in the private label product business can vary widely based on several factors:

Product Selection: The type of products you choose to private label can greatly impact your income potential. High-demand, high-margin products tend to yield higher profits.

Supplier Negotiation: Your ability to negotiate favorable terms with suppliers can affect your profit margins.

Marketing and Promotion: Effective marketing efforts can lead to more sales and increased income.

Market Demand: The demand for your private label products plays a significant role in determining your profit potential.

Efficiency: Your ability to efficiently manage inventory, fulfill orders, and provide excellent customer service can impact your overall income.

Successful private label product entrepreneurs could earn anywhere from a few hundred to several thousand dollars per month or more, depending on the factors mentioned above. Exceptional entrepreneurs who excel in product selection, branding, marketing, and efficient operations can achieve significant income.

Private label products offer an entrepreneurial opportunity for individuals looking to build their own brands and create profitable businesses. While it comes with challenges, those who excel in product selection, supplier relationships, branding, and marketing can establish successful private label businesses. Success often involves ongoing market research, innovation, and a commitment to delivering quality products that resonate with customers under your unique brand.

Navigating the Digital Landscape: A Guide to Becoming a Social Media Specialist

In the age of connectivity, social media has become an integral part of our personal lives and a cornerstone of modern business marketing. Social media specialists play a crucial role in helping businesses and individuals harness the power of these platforms to build their brands and engage with audiences. If you're interested in becoming a social media specialist, this guide will provide insights into the role, key considerations, potential challenges, and the pay range associated with this dynamic career.

Understanding the Role of a Social Media Specialist

A social media specialist is responsible for managing and implementing social media marketing strategies on behalf of clients or organizations. Their key responsibilities include:

1. Content Creation: Creating engaging and relevant content for various social media platforms, including text, images, videos, and infographics.

2. Strategy Development: Developing comprehensive social media strategies aligned with the client's goals, target audience, and brand identity.

3. Platform Management: Managing and maintaining active social media accounts on platforms such as Facebook, Instagram, Twitter, LinkedIn, and TikTok.

4. Engagement: Interacting with followers, responding to comments and messages, and fostering a sense of community around the brand.

5. Analytics and Reporting: Tracking and analyzing key performance metrics to assess the effectiveness of social media campaigns and making data-driven decisions for improvement.

6. Advertising: Running paid social media advertising campaigns to increase brand visibility and reach a wider audience.

Steps to Becoming a Social Media Specialist

1. Education and Training:

While a formal degree in marketing, communications, or a related field is beneficial, practical experience and continuous learning are equally important.

2. Gaining Experience:

Start by managing your own social media profiles or volunteering to handle social media for a nonprofit or small business.

3. Building a Portfolio:

Create a portfolio showcasing your work, including examples of content creation, campaign management, and analytics reports.

4. Staying Updated:

Stay current with social media trends, algorithm changes, and new platforms by attending webinars, workshops, and industry conferences.

5. Networking:

Build a professional network by connecting with other social media specialists, marketers, and industry professionals.

Challenges and Considerations

Working as a social media specialist can be both rewarding and challenging:

Fast-Paced Environment: Social media is dynamic, with trends and algorithms constantly changing. Keeping up with these changes can be demanding.

Responsibility: Managing a brand's online presence comes with significant responsibility, as your actions can impact the company's reputation.

Measuring ROI: Proving the return on investment (ROI) of social media efforts can be challenging but is essential for clients and employers.

Pay Range for Social Media Specialists

The pay range for social media specialists can vary widely based on several factors:

Experience: Entry-level specialists may earn between $30,000 to $50,000 annually, while experienced specialists with several years of experience and a proven track record can earn $50,000 to $100,000 or more per year.

Location: Salaries can differ significantly based on the cost of living in your region. Specialists in major cities may earn higher salaries than those in smaller towns.

Industry and Company Size: Social media specialists working for large corporations or agencies may earn more than those at small businesses or startups.

Skills and Specialization: Specialists with skills in paid advertising, influencer marketing, or specific platforms like Facebook or Instagram may command higher salaries.

The median annual salary for social media specialists in the United States was around $50,000 to $60,000. However, salaries can vary widely based on the factors mentioned above.

Becoming a social media specialist offers an exciting career path for individuals with a passion for digital marketing and social media platforms. It's a role that requires a combination of creativity, analytical skills, and adaptability to navigate the ever-evolving world of social media. With the right education, experience, and dedication, you can build a rewarding career as a social media specialist and help businesses thrive in the digital age.

FREELANCE EDITING

Crafting Stories Through Pixels: A Guide to Freelance Video Editing

Freelance video editing is a dynamic and creative profession that allows talented individuals to transform raw footage into captivating visual stories. If you're considering a career as a freelance video editor, this guide will provide insights into the role, key considerations, potential challenges, and the pay range associated with this exciting field.

Understanding the Role of a Freelance Video Editor

A freelance video editor is a professional who specializes in the post-production process of video content. Their primary responsibilities include:

1. **Footage Review:** Reviewing and organizing raw video footage and audio files.

2. **Editing:** Assembling and trimming video clips, adding transitions, special effects, and animations, and adjusting audio levels to create a coherent and visually appealing story.

3. **Color Grading:** Enhancing the visual aesthetics of the video through color correction and grading techniques.

4. **Audio Enhancement:** Cleaning up audio, adding sound effects, music, and ensuring clear and balanced audio quality.

5. **Collaboration:** Collaborating with clients, directors, and other team members to achieve the desired video outcome.

6. **Software Proficiency:** Utilizing video editing software such as Adobe Premiere Pro, Final Cut Pro, DaVinci Resolve, or other industry-standard tools.

Steps to Becoming a Freelance Video Editor

1. Education and Training:

Many video editors begin by pursuing a degree or certification in film editing, multimedia, or a related field. However, practical experience and a strong portfolio are equally crucial.

2. Building a Portfolio:

Create a portfolio that showcases your editing skills and style. Include a variety of projects, such as short films, commercials, or personal projects.

3. Networking:

Connect with fellow videographers, filmmakers, and potential clients through industry events, social media, and online platforms.

4. Gaining Experience:

Start by taking on small projects to build your experience and reputation. As your skills grow, you can tackle more substantial projects.

5. Marketing Yourself:

Establish an online presence through a professional website or social media profiles to attract potential clients.

Challenges and Considerations

Working as a freelance video editor comes with its set of challenges:

Client Expectations: Meeting and managing client expectations, including revisions and feedback, can be demanding.

Competition: The field of video editing is competitive, and staying ahead often requires continuous learning and honing of skills.

Tight Deadlines: Meeting tight deadlines while maintaining quality can be challenging in the fast-paced world of media production.

Pay Range for Freelance Video Editors

The pay range for freelance video editors varies based on several factors:

Experience: Entry-level video editors may charge anywhere from $15 to $30 per hour, while experienced editors with a strong portfolio can command rates of $50 to $100 or more per hour.

Project Complexity: Rates can vary depending on the complexity of the project, including the length of the video, the quality of footage, and the extent of post-production work required.

Client and Industry: Rates may differ based on the client's budget and the industry. Corporate clients may have different budgets than independent filmmakers.

Location: Rates can vary significantly based on your geographic location and the cost of living in that area.

Freelance video editors in the United States earned an average hourly rate ranging from $30 to $75 per hour, with variation based on the factors mentioned above.

Freelance video editing offers a rewarding career path for individuals passionate about visual storytelling and post-production. It's a profession that allows you to unleash your creativity, work on diverse projects, and collaborate with talented professionals across the media industry. By building a strong portfolio, honing your skills, and effectively marketing your services, you can establish yourself as a successful freelance video editor and embark on a fulfilling journey in the world of visual storytelling.

START A VENDING MACHINE BUSINESS

Unlocking Profit Potential: A Guide to Starting a Vending Machine Business

The world of entrepreneurship is filled with diverse opportunities, and one of the lesser-explored but potentially lucrative avenues is the vending machine business. If you're considering delving into this realm, this guide will provide you with insights into the process, key considerations, potential challenges, and the pay range associated with starting and operating a vending machine business.

Understanding the Vending Machine Business

A vending machine business involves the following key steps:

1. Market Research:

Identify the target market and location for your vending machines. Understanding your potential customers is crucial for success.

2. Machine Selection:

Choose the types of vending machines and products you want to offer. Options range from snacks and beverages to specialized products like toiletries or electronics.

3. Supplier Relations:

Establish relationships with suppliers to source products at competitive prices and maintain a reliable inventory.

4. Location Acquisition:

Secure suitable locations for your vending machines. High-traffic areas with a consistent flow of potential customers are ideal.

5. Machine Installation:

Install and maintain your vending machines, ensuring they are fully operational and well-stocked at all times.

6. Pricing Strategy:

Determine the pricing strategy for your products, considering factors like product cost, location, and market rates.

7. Maintenance and Customer Service:

Regularly service and restock your machines, and provide customer support as needed.

Challenges and Considerations

Starting a vending machine business offers several advantages, such as low overhead costs and the potential for passive income. However, it also comes with its set of challenges:

Location Challenges: Finding and securing high-traffic locations can be competitive and may require negotiation or ongoing fees.

Maintenance and Restocking: Regular maintenance and restocking can be time-consuming, especially if you have multiple machines in different locations.

Market Competition: Depending on your chosen niche and location, you may face competition from other vending machine operators.

Pay Range in the Vending Machine Business

The pay range in the vending machine business can vary based on several factors:

Location: The profitability of vending machines heavily depends on location. Machines placed in busy areas with high foot traffic tend to generate higher income.

Product Selection: The type of products you offer can impact your earnings. Snacks, beverages, and popular items often have a steady demand.

Pricing Strategy: Your pricing strategy and profit margin per product influence your overall income.

Number of Machines: Owning multiple machines can increase your potential income, but it also comes with greater operational responsibilities.

Operating Costs: Expenses like restocking, maintenance, and lease fees can affect your profitability.

Vending machine operators could earn anywhere from a few hundred to several thousand dollars per month per machine, depending on the factors mentioned above. Successful operators with multiple well-placed machines in high-traffic areas could achieve significant income.

Starting a vending machine business can be a rewarding endeavor, offering opportunities for passive income and business ownership. With careful planning, effective location selection, and a well-thought-out product strategy, you can build a vending machine business that generates steady income over time. While it may require effort and dedication to manage and grow, a vending machine business can be a valuable addition to your entrepreneurial portfolio and a path to financial success.